# *Toon on Top*

## The full story of Newcastle United's dramatic '94-'95 Season

Compiled by
**DAVID EMERY**

# SIMON & SCHUSTER
LONDON · SYDNEY · NEW YORK · TOKYO · TORONTO

First published in Great Britain by Simon & Schuster Ltd, 1995
A Viacom Company

Simon & Schuster Ltd
West Garden Place
Kendal Street
London W2 2AQ

Simon & Schuster of Australia Pty Ltd
Sydney

A CIP catalogue record for this book is available from the British
Library.

ISBN 0-671-51181-5

Typeset by The Imaging Business

Printed and bound in Great Britain by
HarperCollins*Manufacturing*.

For news, reports and independent information on
Newcastle United in the 1995/1996 season call
**0891-137-221**

For all the news throughout the 1995/96 soccer season
call the Daily Express Soccer line 0891-204-270
calls cost 39p per minute cheap rate
and 49p per minute at all other times

Prices correct at time of going to press

# Contents

# *Foreword*

When I walk into St. James' Park these days it is a wondrous sight. A truly magnificent stadium is in the process of getting the team it and Geordieland deserve.

I cannot help casting my mind back to 1947 when I was signed as a full-time pro to play for the club I love. This, of course, was in the days of the maximum wage, when we played in front of crowds of 50-60,000 but suffered the restraints of the time. No player got more than the £20 a week they were entitled to receive although there were little bits of bonuses for FA Cup success: £50 a man to win the competition; nothing at all for coming second.

So excuse me if I notice a few differences around the old place. These days players have rightly established a certain status. In the old days it was not quite like that. Never mind the wages, we didn't wear all the smart training gear they have now. The trainer would throw a pile of shirts on the dressing-room table and we would fight to get the best one.

We used to get two tickets for the match, but players' wives received no favours. They would have to stand outside the ground to meet us after a game. Nowadays they even have a creche in the ground. But this different world is a godsend to Newcastle supporters.

When I think about the way the club has been turned around under the control of Sir John Hall and Kevin Keegan, it is incredible. It is only a few seasons ago since Newcastle United looked as though they were heading for the old Second Division. I remember being in the ground that season and you could feel the despair. What was the future? There didn't seem to be one.

Fans now have been waiting so long for a little bit of success. Kevin Keegan is giving them that and I am sure it is going to continue. Whether it is this year, next year, or whenever, I am sure he is going to win the title. And I would love to be a player involved in that because running out at St. James' Park in front of a full house makes the hair stand up on the back of your neck.

Like every other black-and-white, I was disappointed United didn't make it to Wembley in 1995 and bring the FA Cup home. I am proud to be a member of the last Newcastle side to do it in 1955. Forty years is big gap and like a lot of fans I thought the wait was over. Would it

have been different if Andy Cole had not been sold? We will never
know. I would not want to criticise Kevin in view of the outstanding
work he has done in such as short time, but I did question the wisdom
of that sale, particularly as Cole was sold to a a major rival.

In Kevin Keegan Newcastle have a manager who will lead the club
all the way to the top and I am excited about what is around the corner for Newcastle. My message is simply this: make sure you keep
Keegan. He is your inspiration. He already has some very good players, an outstanding example of which is Peter Beardsley who was a
young player with me when I managed Carlisle. He will get more
good players. The result will be that Newcastle will become bigger,
better and altogether more successful in the trophy-winning business.

*Bob Stokoe, a member of
Newcastle's last FA Cup
winning team. His career
spanned 13 years starting
in 1947.*

# Then and Now

Kevin Keegan's second coming at St James' Park has been soccer's equivalent of the Industrial Revolution.

When that swept into Tyneside during the 1870s it brought coal mines, heavy engineering works and the birth of football. Now Keegan's boundless enthusiasm and tactical astuteness have revitalised an area bursting with tradition and ancient achievements. Newcastle United have enjoyed three great eras: as kings of Edwardian football from 1904-1911; Hughie Gallacher's League champions of 1927; and Jackie Milburn's Wembley wonders of the Fifties.

They have seen the advent of Supermac Malcolm Macdonald in the Seventies, the arrival of Keegan as Arthur Cox's master-signing in the promotion team of 1984. Now the second coming of Keegan could signal a return to the glory days, the roots of which were laid back in the latter half of the last century.

Then the spread of heavy machinery took men out of the fields and into the factories, thousands of them working and playing side by side in huge conglomerations of manpower.

Football was the new game sweeping the nation and nowhere was it embraced more eagerly than in Newcastle. Two teams were formed: Newcastle East End and Newcastle West End. Both started in 1882 but West End were the senior by two months, originating in the October of that year and operating on a ground called St James' Park. East End were based in Byker before moving to Chillingham Road in Heaton.

Both clubs competed in the Northern League but West End carried more clout through an influential local businessman John Black. Thanks to his financial help they were able to sign two Scottish internationals, left winger Ralph Aitken and midfield man Bob Kelso.

East End, though, were ambitious. First they lured away West End's manager Tom Watson; then, in 1890, they became a limited company, issuing 2,000 shares at 10 shillings a time. In 1891-92 the rivals met five times and East End won all five: 2-0, 3-0, 4-0, 3-0 and 7-1.

West End were in a mess and on the brink of calling it a day when, in an inspired meeting in the spring of 1892, the two clubs met at the home of director Joe Bell and came to an historic agreement.

West End folded and East End moved to St James' Park. The colours were already established. East End had played in blue, then red and now black and white stripes. East End reigned supreme but support was still meagre, so in December 1892 a meeting was called at Bath Lane Hall to decide how to inject more passion into the club. They decided a new name was needed and, after a heated debate in which Newcastle Rangers and Newcastle City were seriously considered, they settled for Newcastle United. Within six months United were elected to the Second Division of the Football League. Funds were scarce and the directors had to have a whip round of £2 10s each before they could travel to London and fulfil their first fixture against another new club, Woolwich Arsenal. On September 2 1893 Newcastle United played Arsenal and goals by Tom Crate and Jack Sorley gave them a 2-2 draw.

Newcastle's first home League game was also against Arsenal and this time, in front of a 2,000 crowd, they won 6-0 with hat-tricks from the Scot Joe Wallace and Willie Thompson. A Dominican friar reputedly helped to stir up the crowd in his black and white habit and this convinced the club they should adopt those colours. "H'away the Lads," yelled the crowd for the first time. And H'away they went.

In 1895 Newcastle made perhaps the most important signing in their history. They took on Frank Watt, the former club secretary of Dundee United, a man known for his innovative thinking and massive handlebar moustache. At St James' Watt was also called secretary, but he was far more than that. He was a one-man task force who worked night and day to transform Newcastle into the kings of Edwardian football.

Watt, "The Guv'nor" as he was known, drafted in a platoon of players, many from his native Scotland. They were men he had assessed as possessing not only rare skills but an exceptional will to win. Bob Foyers from St Bernards became captain; "Gentleman" James Howie, from Ayrshire, joined in 1902 – wing-half Peter McWilliam – "Peter the Great" from Inverness arrived the following year and in 1904 Watt engineered the most audacious coup of all, buying another Inverness man, right-back Andy McCombie, from rivals Sunderland for the then unheard-of fee of £700.

Under Watt Newcastle played in the 2-3-5 formation considered the norm by all major clubs but they brought one significant change: they believed in short passing, moving in groups up the field, a precursor to Arthur Rowe's push-and-run Spurs and the famed triangles of the greatest Liverpool teams.

It was a system which served them well, allowing the free-scoring wingers Jock Rutherford and tiny Albert Gosnell to reach menacing positions with support around them and servicing a centre-forward Bill Appleyard, a former Grimsby trawlerman, who brought his near-14 stone into the opposition penalty area with crushing effect.

The durability of Newcastle was embodied by their goalkeeper, the Scottish international James Lawrence. At a time when goalkeepers were afforded little or no protection and were expected to collect some hefty knocks from opposing centre-forwards as a matter of course, Lawrence did not miss a match for six seasons. In all he stayed for 18 years, making 505 appearances, including 432 in the League.

Together with Rutherford and the England captain Colin Veitch, Lawrence played in all three Championship sides and five FA Cup finals in that wonderful era for the Magpies between 1904 and 1911. But for their row of Cup disasters Newcastle would have set records which would surely have remained out of reach for all time. How they did not achieve the double during this period remains one of football's greatest mysteries.

In 1905 they won the First Division for the first time, beating Middlesbrough on the last day of the season 3-0 at Ayresome Park to clinch the title. A mighty Appleyard header set them on their way followed by goals from Ronnie Orr and Rutherford.

The double beckoned as they travelled to Crystal Palace to meet Aston Villa, hundreds of Geordie fans travelling down in boats on the North Sea to marvel at the huge glass exhibition palace which overlooked the stadium. A crowd of 101,117 saw the Magpies well beaten through two goals from Aston Villa's buccaneering centre-forward Harry Hampton. If defeat was bitter, it was sweetened by the cascades of money. St James' was developed at a cost of £12,000 to become one of the premier stadiums in the country. Capacity was increased to 52,500 with a new west stand holding almost 5,000.

The following year Newcastle finished fourth in the League and again reached the Cup final, this time losing a close-fought tussle to Andy Young's 75th minute winner.

In 1907 the League title went back to Newcastle yet they went out of the Cup to non-League opposition in the first round. In 1908 they were fourth in the League and beaten again in the Cup final, 3-1 to Wolverhampton Wanderers although they had the satisfaction of seeing Jimmy Howie score their first goal in a final.

So it went on. In 1909 they were League champions but more Cup disaster came in a semi-final defeat by Manchester United. In 1910 they finally won the Cup, beating lowly Barnsley 2-0 at Goodison Park after drawing at Crystal Palace. In the process Albert Shepherd won, and scored, the first penalty awarded in an FA Cup final. Normal service was resumed in 1910 when they lost the final once more, again after a replay, to Bradford City.

In five finals at Crystal Palace Newcastle did not win one game. The theory at the time was that they did not, or could not, adjust their accurate passing game from the bare surface of St James' Park to the longer, thicker grass of Crystal Palace. Indeed, the very thought of Crystal Palace clearly unnerved Newcastle, for the name of that non-League club who had beaten them in the Cup in 1907 was ... Crystal Palace. Generations of Newcastle successors had less trouble with the thick pile of the Wembley turf. That ground became a lucky charm with the Magpies winning the Cup in 1924, 1932, 1951, 1952 and 1955 before Liverpool broke the run by beating them in 1974.

It was after Newcastle's 1924 success that football modified the off-side law in what was to be the most important rule change of them all. Much of that was due to Newcastle's FA Cup winning captain Frank Hudspeth.

Hudspeth was a disciple of Billy McCracken, the great Irish full back who possessed one of the finest tactical footballing brains of the early 20th century. He quickly learned how to play opponents offside with the cleaness of the whistle that inevitably followed his moves.

The law as it stood decreed that a player was offside unless there were three players including the goalkeeper between him and his opponents' goal when the ball was last played. McCracken saw this as a way of stifling attacks at the half-way line. The full backs simply moved forward and the practice threatened to kill football's appeal.

It was the Scots, speaking with powerful authority in the councils of the game, who proposed the change at a meeting of the International Football Federation in 1925. The number of players between the attacking player and goal was reduced to two. The game was immediately handed back to the attackers. The following season 6,373 goals were scored in the Football League compared with 4,700 the season before. The Cup victory of 1924 was obtained by a decent, hard-working Newcastle side, but one which did not suggest the brilliance which was to unfold at St James' two years later.

The First World War had put an effective full-stop at the end of United's first glorious charge. Steady evolution rather than revolution was the watchword when League football resumed.

Newcastle found two fine defensive players in Hudspeth and Charlie Spencer and the man who would become known as Mr Newcastle, Stan Seymour.

United's route to Wembley was one of dogged determination with three replays needed to get past Derby County. Their final opponents were Aston Villa whom they met in a League match shortly before the big day. United played a virtual reserve team then to safeguard their players but the plan backfired with goalkeeper Sandy Mutch, only one of two regulars on show, being injured and missing Wembley.

His stand-in Bill Bradley went on to have a magnificent game in a team which included 42-year-old full-back Billy Hampson, the oldest player to appear in a final. Goals by Neil Harris and Seymour clinched a 2-0 win. Wembley had been conquered for the first time and once again the money generated by the success would be spent with devastating effectiveness.

It brought to Newcastle one of the greatest geniuses of the game, the 5ft 5in Hughie Kilpatrick Gallacher, a Scottish goalscoring phenomenon who was to illuminate Tyneside as he sped across their soccer firmament like a shooting star.

At 22 Gallacher was already a legend in Scotland where he had scored 65 League goals in 66 games for Airdrie, plus five goals in his first four Scottish internationals. Airdrie fans were wild when they heard of Newcastle's interest but Frank Watt made the signing of Gallacher his last great gift to Newcastle.

What a gift it was. Gallacher was to score 143 goals in 174 appearances for the club which makes him their fourth all-time leading marksman behind Jackie Milburn (238), Albert Stubbins (237) and Len White (153). His strike rate was nothing short of sensational. He scored twice on his debut, against Everton on December 12, 1925, and went on to hit 25 goals in 22 games that season.

He was fast, elusive, strong on the ball despite his size and possessed dazzling footwork. The following year he inspired the surge to the championship.

Newcastle's forward line were the mighty midgets with an average height of 5ft 6in, yet the team scored 96 goals, the most in the First Division, and conceded 58, the fewest. The change in the offside rule was taking huge effect and Newcastle's brilliant solution was to convert wing half Spencer into the game's first real centre-half. With a 3-2-5 formation United found they could contain attackers while losing none of their potency up front.

Newcastle averaged three goals a game at home. Gallacher led the way with 26 goals in 21 games at St James' Park and 39 overall, a record that was to stand until Andy Cole beat it in 1993/94. Newcastle's gates averaged 35,000, including a record 67,211 who saw them beat Sunderland at Easter. Gallacher (who else?) scored the vital goal.

Newcastle never burned so brightly again in the Twenties although Gallacher kept banging in the goals and two years later his tally of 34 staved off relegation. In 1930 Gallacher, who had a quick temper to match his quick feet, fell out with Newcastle manager Andy Cunningham and was sold to Chelsea for £10,000. When Chelsea next came to St James' 68,386 packed the ground, with 10,000 locked outside, to say farewell to their Scottish hero.

In 1932 Newcastle again displayed their liking for Wembley, beating Arsenal with the help of the most controversial goal scored in a Cup final. Arsenal were seemingly unbeatable, with a stable of stars like Cliff Bastin, David Jack and Eddie Hapgood. Alex James was missing through injury but the key man was to be referee Percy Harper.

Arsenal went ahead through Bob John but then Newcastle sent inside-right Jimmy Richardson chasing a long pass down the wing. The ball looked to have crossed the goal-line before he reached it but he whipped it over anyway and centre-forward Jack Allen flicked it home. Hapgood, who had been marking Allen, had run across the line when he thought the ball was out. What pictorial evidence there is and the views of those on the line seem to support Arsenal but the game had swung. Allen scored his second off a post and Jimmy Nelson collected the Cup from Queen Mary.

It was to be almost 20 years before Newcastle fans were to sing *Blaydon Races* at Wembley again. And then it was to herald the most remarkable Cup-winning sequence of the post-war years. It was a golden age for football with spectators flocking to forget the horrors of Hitler. During the war Tom Finney and Stan Mortensen guested for the Magpies. In 1946-47 Newcastle boasted a forward line that was the equal of any in England.

There was left-winger Tommy Pearson who played for both Scotland and England, centre-forward Charlie Wayman who scored more than 250 goals in his career, Roy Bentley at inside-right and, at inside-left, Len Shackleton who cost United a record £13,050 from Bradford. Shackleton made a spectacular debut, scoring six times against Newport, including three in five minutes, as United equalled the record League victory of 13-0.

Newcastle also had a promising right-winger who had scored six goals in the first half of his trial game and who was soon to move to centre-forward and become their greatest hero of all: Jackie Milburn. His switch coincided with a rise in the great club's fortunes.

In 1947-48 United ended a 15-year absence from the First Division by winning promotion. Their smallest crowd for a Second Division match that season was 43,000. Next season they averaged 56,299 and Milburn was the man they all wanted to see.

He had scored 20 goals in the promotion season and was now ready to blossom. Behind him was Joe Harvey, bringing his qualities as an ex-sergeant-major to bear as captain, and "Rock of Gibraltar" Frank Brennan at the heart of defence, all 6ft 3in and 14 stone of him. (Brennan's breakfast was legendary; seven eggs and eight rashers of bacon). The Scottish winger Bobby Mitchell joined for £16,000 in 1949 and 44,000 turned out to watch his debut in a friendly against Liverpool.

In early spring they were on course to win the double. They stood fourth in the League seven points behind Tottenham with four games in hand (two points per game then) and had just beaten Wolves 2-1 in the Cup semi-final. But thoughts of Wembley clouded their League ambition, they failed to win any of their next eight League games and finished fourth.

The Cup final was a different proposition. Against a Blackpool side boasting Stanley Matthews and Stan Mortensen Newcastle were irresistible. And it was the famed speed of Milburn that set up a famous victory. In the 50th minute he exploded on to a George Robledo through ball, raced 40 yards and threaded his shot past George Farm.

Four minutes later Milburn added the finest goal of his season, perhaps the best of his career and one which was immediately lauded as the greatest goal seen at a Wembley Cup final. It was begun by Tommy Walker, a qualified lay preacher, who showed his meaner streak by beating two Blackpool players in a brilliant run before passing inside to little "Tom Thumb" Ernie Taylor. The 5ft 4in inside-forward, a player with gifts before his time, laid the perfect back-heel into Milburn's powerful path and the striker hit a thunderous drive into the back of the net from 30 yards

Taylor went on to gain FA Cup finalist medals with three separate clubs. Five months after his Wembley appearance with Newcastle he had joined Blackpool for £25,000 and played in their remarkable 1953 defeat of Bolton, the Matthews Final. Then he joined Manchester United after the Munich tragedy and was in their team beaten 2-0 by Bolton in 1958.

When Newcastle began their defence of the Cup the following season it was the turn of Mitchell to shine. Newcastle were struggling in a third-round tie with Villa, losing 2-1, when Mitchell's brilliance took over. He scored twice to turn the game and set Newcastle back on course to a Wembley showdown with Arsenal.

In all, Mitchell scored 113 goals in 12 years at St James', none more vital than the penalty he converted in the semi-final against Blackburn Rovers that year. Newcastle had had a tough time throughout the Cup run, drawn against four clubs from the top six of the First Division and at home only once. Blackburn took them to a replay at Elland Road and only moments remained of a tense match when Mitchell stepped up to take the penalty.

Arsenal were attempting the first double of the 20th century when they arrived at Wembley to face a Newcastle team which had remained unchanged throughout all seven Cup matches. This time Mitchell was content to be playmaker with the Chilean winger George Robledo the match winner.

George and his brother Ted had settled in England after their parents fled the 1932 revolution in their home country. In 1949 they were signed from Barnsley in a joint deal worth £26,500. Two years later George equalled Hughie Gallacher's record of 39 goals in a season and went on to score 91 from 164 games overall.

None was as memorable as the one he claimed in the 1952 final after Mitchell's 84th-minute jinking run down the touchline. Mitchell crossed to the far post and there was Robledo meeting the ball to head past George Swindin and via a post into the net. With Ted also in the team, Newcastle that day fielded two Chileans, three Scots, an Irishman, a Welshman and four Englishmen.

As Harvey collected the Cup from Winston Churchill, Newcastle fans celebrated the first back-to-back Cup victories since Blackburn in 1891. Three years later they were celebrating again, but not before they had suffered enough shocks to last them a lifetime.

They needed three tough matches to get past Nottingham Forest and then in the semi-final found themselves facing York City, the giant-killing sensations of the competition. The plucky little Yorkshire side held Newcastle to a draw but in the replay the Magpies were on their way to Wembley again when Len White hit the crucial goal.

Newcastle's Wembley team to face Manchester City included Bob Stokoe, whose other great Wembley day was to come as manager of Sunderland in the Cup final some 20 years later. Stokoe regarded Milburn as "the most exciting thing I have seen on a football field" and Wor Jackie showed why in explosive fashion within 45 seconds of the match beginning.

White sent over a corner and Milburn, standing just beyond the penalty spot bulleted a header into the top corner of the net. It was the quickest goal scored at Wembley and became one of the most famous soccer photographs. Bobby Johnstone equalised for City but then in a storming finish Mitchell scored himself and set up another for George Hannah. For the third time in five years Newcastle lifted the Cup, this time captain Jimmy Scoular taking the trophy from Queen Elizabeth II.

City's heroic German goalkeeper Bert Trautmann, a former prisoner of war, was later found to have broken a small bone in his neck during the match, but there was no doubting whom the Geordie fans saw as the star of the show: John Edward Thompson Milburn, whose initials JET could hardly have been more apposite for his goal that day.

Milburn, born in Ashington, left Newcastle in 1957 after scoring 177 league goals in 353 appearances. He remained the quintessential Geordie hero, the yardstick by which all future heroes, even Kevin Keegan, would be judged. More than 46,000 packed St James' for his testimonial in 1967; almost 100,000 were on the streets for his funeral 20 years later.

The departure of Milburn to become player-manager of Linfield heralded a decline for Newcastle and a new manager, Charlie Mitten, was introduced to halt the slide. Mitten proved a fine judge of a player, bringing in Ivor Allchurch, the young god of Welsh football, and the slim, fair-haired George Eastham. Yet for all his talented inside-forwards and for all the goal-scoring qualities of White, Mitten was unable to prevent Newcastle being relegated in 1961.

Mitten went but he had left a legacy and in 1962 Newcastle won the FA Youth Cup with a team including Bobby Moncur, David Craig and Alan Suddick. By then the board had persuaded their former captain and legendary hard man Joe Harvey to return as manager. It was a fine choice. Harvey proved as effective a manager as captain and set about rebuilding the Magpies.

He bought Trevor Hockey from Nottingham Forest, Gordon Marshall from Hearts and another Scot, Dave Hilley. Harvey built his team from the back in practical fashion to meet the needs of contemporary football which had become meaner and more defence-minded. Craig and the young Frank Clark were outstanding in the United team which gained promotion in 1964-65, as were the wing-half Stan Anderson who arrived from Roker and the big centre-half John McGrath. Jim Iley from Forest was left-half and Bryan "Pop" Robson a lively prospect up front.

In his fine book *Toons of Glory* (Souvenir Press) Joe Bernstein says Harvey went on to assemble arguably the strongest defence in the club's history: goalkeeper Iam McFaul, Craig, Clark and Moncur, the captain. But his attack did not flourish similarly. Ron McGarry, a bustling centre-forward, was injury prone and in their first season back in the top flight, 50 goals in 42 League games saw Newcastle finish 15th. The following season Newcastle scored only 39 even though Suddick had matured into a brilliant all-round footballer with immense power in his shooting.

Harvey took drastic action. He sold Suddick to Blackpool in 1966 for £60,000 to finance the purchase of Dave McNamee, Dave Elliott and Tommy Robson. It also gave him the start-up money to pursue the one player he needed more than any other: a replacement for Wor Jackie, a goal-scoring centre-forward.

Harvey knew who he wanted. It was big Wyn Davies, the Welshman who led the line at Bolton Wanderers and was reputedly the best header of the ball since Tommy Lawton. Davies insisted on relating all details of the proposed transfer down the phone to his Welsh mother but finally, in October 1966, Harvey had his man for a club record £80,000.

"You ain't seen nothing like the mighty Wyn," sang the Geordie fans who turned up in their tens of thousands to hail Harvey's team and give him the financial muscle to continue his transfer activity. Jackie Sinclair, from Leicester, cost £70,000 and Jim Scott arrived from Hibernian for £40,000. Pop Robson linked telepathically with Davies and suddenly Newcastle were scoring goals again they finished 10th in the First Division.

They also qualified for Europe under the prevailing Fairs Cup rules which allowed only one team from each city. The critics scoffed. How would Newcastle, scraping in as the fourth-rank representatives for England, live with some of the European giants?

In the event the Magpies took Europe by storm. They won the cup (now the Uefa Cup) at their first attempt and in three years in the competition lost only two ties from 12, one on away goals, the other on penalties. Feyenoord, Inter Milan, Sporting Lisbon, FC Porto, Real Zaragoza, Ujpest Dozsa and Glasgow Rangers were all sent packing from St James' Park. Dutch aces Feyenoord were the first to feel the lash, losing 4-0. Next came Sporting Lisbon and ready for them was a crowd of 54,000 and Pop Robson who volleyed one of the finest goals seen at the old stadium.

Real Zaragoza were dispatched in the next round, thanks to the Robson-Davies combination, and another Portuguese team, Setubal, fell in the quarter-final. Now Newcastle had to face Glasgow Rangers and a Fairs Cup record crowd of 75,580 at Ibrox. It was goalkeeper McFaul's finest hour, diving to save Andy Penman's penalty to keep the score-sheet clean. In the return at St James' Newcastle took a 2-0 lead through Scott and Sinclair, sparking a massed pitch invasion from the Scottish supporters which delayed play for 17 minutes.

McFaul had another superb game in the final against Hungarians Ujpest Dozsa, who fielded seven internationals and had beaten Leeds in the quarter-finals. Newcastle thrashed them 3-0 in an outstanding performance that included two goals from Moncur.

Disaster loomed in the return leg, as Newcastle trailed 2-0 before half-time, but an inspired team-talk by Harvey, who exhorted his men to remember the Geordie spirit, carried them to an extraordinary fight-back.

Moncur began it with a real captain's goal from a corner, the Danish international Ben Arentoft levelled the scores and finally young Alan Foggon, on as a substitute, ran from the half-way line before hitting a 20-yard shot against the bar. The ball rebounded and Foggon, following up, slid it home. The Fairs Cup was on its way to Newcastle, on a 6-2 aggregate scoreline, and Moncur had scored three of them. In his 343-game career with Newcastle he was to score only five others.

No one embodied the never-say-die spirit of Newcastle more than Wyn Davies. He had smashed his cheek-bone in the first leg against the Hungarians but refused to have an operation which would have kept him out of the return. His contribution on an emotional night was immense.

Newcastle's European adventure continued the following season. With the help of a new £100,000 signing "Jinky" Jimmy Smith they went on to beat Dundee, FC Porto and Southampton before falling to Anderlecht in the quarter-finals on away goals when the Belgians scored in the final minute.

Newcastle were back in the Fairs Cup for the third time the following season, beating an Inter Milan team containing World Cup stars Bonisegna and Mazzola 3-1 on aggregate. The match at St James' was remarkable for the sending-off of the Italian goalkeeper who took exception to the referee and felled him with a single punch.

United's exit in the following round was an anti-climax, beaten on penalties by Pecsi Dozsa. It was to be seven years before their next appearance in Europe.

The season of 1971 brought the horrific 2-1 FA Cup defeat by Hereford but also the arrival of Supermac. Davies had had his day and Harvey, ever pragmatic, was quickly on the phone to Alec Stock at Luton. Stock had converted a young Fulham full-back into a muscular scoring machine who was fast becoming the sensation of Kenilworth Road with his explosive running and powerful shooting. The asking price was £180,000. Harvey paid and the 21-year-old Malcolm Macdonald arrived at St James' by Rolls Royce.

It was to be the perfect marriage, the brash Macdonald who wanted only to score goals and the Geordie fans who craved another No. 9 to idolise. Macdonald did not take long to impress them, hitting a hat-trick against Liverpool on his home debut. He went on to score 95 goals in 187 games for United and win a club record 14 England caps before a dispute with new manager Gordon Lee, an avowed enemy of the star system, saw him leave for Arsenal.

For the moment, though, the good times were returning. Terry Hibbitt joined from Leeds, at £30,000 a fraction of Macdonald's price but a player of immense influence, and Harvey splashed out £150,000 for Blackpool's Scottish international midfield genius Tony Green.

Green was to be the final piece in an exciting jigsaw, a player of sublime talent and withering pace. But in September 1972 at Selhurst Park, Green stepped into a divot and turned his ankle so badly that he tore knee ligaments. The injury was to cost him his career after only 35 games with Newcastle.

Still Harvey's team carried enough commitment and charisma to charge their way to the FA Cup final. Macdonald had formed a lethal partnership up front with John Tudor. Behind them they had Jinky Jimmy and Tommy Cassidy, a young Irishman Harvey had snapped up from Glentoran for £25,000. In the centre of defence Pat Howard partnered Moncur, now nudging 30, and Howard was responsible for the drama that threatened to disrail United's Cup run in the sixth round against Nottingham Forest.

United were losing 2-1 when Craig was judged to have brought down Duncan McKenzie in the penalty area. Howard disputed the decision so vehemently he was sent off, sparking a pitch invasion by Geordie fans which lasted eight minutes. With the penalty converted, Newcastle trailed 3-1 but then began another typical fight-back which took them 4-3 ahead through a Moncur volley.

The FA ordered a re-match because of the crowd trouble and the teams battled to a goalless draw. They met for a third time and a strike from Macdonald finally settled it. Hibbitt and Macdonald combined to score a wonderful goal that ended Burnley's resistance in the semi-final and then it was Wembley again and Liverpool.

An injury to Craig gave a place at full-back to Alan Kennedy who, together with Terry McDermott, a signing from Bury, was to be the man of the match. Both were later to join Liverpool and win a multitude of honours. But this was not their day. Instead it belonged to one

Kevin Keegan, who scored two goals in a 3-0 thrashing.

An estimated 500,000 Geordies still lined the streets for the team's return the next day. But defeat had proved a turning point for Harvey's United. Two years later the Newcastle line-up beaten 2-1 by Manchester City in the League Cup final contained only four of the 1974 team. Macdonald was one of them but his bust-up with Lee was around the corner. Supermac left for London, Lee departed soon afterwards for Everton.

Newcastle turned to a succession of managers to reclaim the former glories. Richard Dinnis arrived, took them into the Uefa Cup and departed. Bill McGarry could not prevent relegation to the Second Division and, despite the purchase of Peter Withe, could not get them out either. Enter Arthur Cox.

Cox had the task of rebuilding Newcastle from the bottom. He was helped by the emergence of Chris Waddle in 1981 but a 6-0 thumping by Chelsea in Cox's second game, followed by a 4-0 FA Cup defeat by little Exeter, showed the depths to which United had sunk. A Messiah was needed, an inspirational figurehead around which to refashion the side. In 1982 Cox found one. He signed Keegan from Southampton for £100,000.

Keegan was 31, nearing the end of a wonderful career that had seen him as King of the Kop at Liverpool and Mighty Mouse of the Bundesliga with Hamburg. But his spirit and commitment were as strong as ever. The fans took to him instantly. They had the hero they craved.

For Keegan's debut against Queens Park Rangers on August 28 1982, they started queuing at 2am. A full-house 35,718 packed the game at kick-off and in *Toons of Glory* Bernstein tells how some supporters raced on to the pitch to kiss Keegan's feet. Newcastle won 1-0, Keegan scored and the *Evening Chronicle* proclaimed on its front page: "Let the Good Times Roll".

And roll they did. With typical forthrightness Keegan threatened to quit at the end of the season unless the team was strengthened. The board got the message and Cox got their backing to bring Peter Beardsley from Canada. David McCreery also signed on and Glenn Roeder was installed to marshall the defence. With Waddle blossoming all the time, the 1983-84 season arrived brimming with promise.

It was no false dawn. Cox had assembled one of the brightest footballing squads in Newcastle's history. There was Jeff Clarke at centre - half, the return of McDermott in midfield and Kevin Carr in goal, the only survivor of Newcastle's previous season in the First Division, 1977-78. Scottish and Newcastle Breweries were encouraged to fund one of the biggest sponsorship deals in football and Keegan kept right on doing his stuff. In McDermott's return match against Rotherham he linked in devastating fashion with Keegan and the little striker notched four goals in a 5-1 win.

Against Manchester City in October it was Beardsley's turn to sparkle in a 5-0 victory. He scored the first hat-trick by a Newcastle player at St James' Park since Alan Gowling in 1976. As the season wore on, Keegan vociferously voiced Beardsley's claims for an England cap, a call that was answered in 1985.

Keegan was full value for his reported £3,000 a week. In 85 appearances he scored 49 goals. More than that, though, he was the soul of Newcastle football. "Kevin never lost the common touch," said Clarke. "That's what made him great."

Keegan announced in February 1984 that he would retire at the end of the season. And he promised that his farewell would coincide with a promotion party. He kept his word, signing off in his 500th and final League match with a goal against Brighton.

The following summer Newcastle took gate receipts of £83,000 for Keegan's testimonial game against Liverpool. He scored from the spot in the 2-2 draw and then departed into the night sky by helicopter.

Keegan's retirement heralded problems for Cox who quarrelled with the board and resigned. In came Jack Charlton, out went Waddle, sold to Spurs. It was the start of a turbulent period for Newcastle, relieved by the emergence of a young, irrepressible midfielder called Paul Gascoigne. Charlton resigned over fan criticism and the board turned to former goalkeeper Iam "Willie" McFaul.

A Brazilian star Mirandinha brought a touch of Copacabana to St James' but still Newcastle seemed incapable of holding on to their own home-grown favourites. Beardsley went to Liverpool for £1.9 million, Gascoigne to Spurs for £2 million. McFaul was unable to survive such transfers and, after a brief caretaker period from Colin Suggett, chairman Gordon McKeag appointed QPR's Jim Smith.

It was a grim time for Newcastle. Jackie Milburn died, then George Robledo, then Joe Harvey. At the end of 1989 Newcastle fell once more into the Second Division.

Again they needed a Messiah. And again Keegan was to be the man. Sir John Hall, the new chairman, appointed Keegan as manager in February 1992 and the sleeping giant was awakened once more. With McDermott installed as his right-hand man, Keegan embarked on an adventure that promises to reap Newcastle's greatest glory. He saved them from relegation in his first season, won the renamed First Division the following year and then in 1993-94 guided them to third in the FA Carling Premiership and a place in Europe. The good times were rolling.

# The
# Matches

# *August 21*

---

### LEICESTER 1

### NEWCASTLE 3

*(Half-time score : 0-0)*

*Leicester:* Ward, Grayson (Roberts 65), Whitlow, Smith, Hill, Mohan, Agnew, Blake (Thompson 65), Draper, Walsh, Joachim.
*Newcastle:* Srnicek, Hottiger, Beresford, Venison, Peacock, Albert, Fox, Lee, Sellars (Elliott 69), Beardsley (Mathie 82), Cole.
*Sub:* Hooper.
*Scorers:* (Leicester): Joachim 90; (United): Cole 51, Beardsley 58, Elliott 74.
*Referee:* M D Reed (Birmingham).
*Attendance*: 20,048

Newcastle hung up the Business As Usual signs at Leicester as Andy Cole and Peter Beardsley pressed the start button on soccer's most prolific scoring production line.

Leicester's worries about the long hard winter in prospect were confirmed at Filbert Street in a match which finished with Newcastle's Pavel Srnicek becoming the first goalkeeper to be sent off in the new Premiership season.

And the glow of victory for Tyneside was followed by genuine concern for Beardsley who left the field clutching his face after a collision with Steve Thompson. The injury was later diagnosed as a fractured cheekbone, which would keep the little sorcerer out of the game for two months.

Srnicek's dismissal came when a late rush of blood sent him careering out to up-end Julian Joachim.

Leicester manager Brian Little must have realised that this first live TV game of the Premiership season confirmed his team are out of their depth even though their new £1.25 million signing Mark Draper had a penalty kick saved. Newcastle, by contrast, demonstrated why they are on so many lists as one of the sides most likely to succeed.

Beardsley and Cole, 65 goals between them last season, inflicted the wounds on Leicester who spent most of the game in their own half on damage-limitation duty.

Newcastle's summer spending spree that brought in World Cup stars Philippe Albert and Marc Hottiger served only to improve Kevin Keegan's options. They were encouraged to join in Newcastle's attacking moves.

The Belgian Albert, scorer of goals against Germany and Holland during the World Cup in America, was booked for trying to con referee Mike Reed into awarding a penalty. But how refreshing it was to see a defender of his ability moving forward with confidence – a throwback to the days when Franz Beckenbauer marauded in similar style. If there was a criticism of Keegan's side it was their over-elaboration around the fringe of the heavily populated Leicester penalty area.

But with Barry Venison taking over the midfield holding role, Paul Bracewell performing so efficiently and Scott Sellars and Ruel Fox holding the flanks, there was a deadly balance to Newcastle.

Robert Lee was able to make damaging runs to set up the clever one-twos which are the hallmark of Newcastle. This was all too much for

Leicester who need pace to go with their tenacity. Only Joachim appears to have the searing explosions of speed which mark out the top players in this elite division.

Leicester defended with concentration in the first half, restricting Newcastle to a 35-yard Albert effort; which Gavin Ward tipped over; and a couple of Beardsley shuffles and shots.

But once Cole broke through in the 51st minute the outcome was inevitable. Beardsley, with one of those darting runs into the box, struck a second goal through Ward's legs. Albert offered City a lifeline when he nudged the disappointing Steve Walsh in the penalty area, Srnicek went the right way to Draper's kick.

Within five minutes of coming on for Sellars, Robbie Elliott wrapped it up with a third goal as Leicester watched for Beardsley and Cole.

The drama of the final minutes came with Beardsley's injury and Srnicek's moment of madness. The goalkeeper had departed for the dressing room when substitute goalkeeper Mike Hooper fumbled a Steve Agnew shot and Joachim scored.

### League Table After Match

|              | P | W | D | L | F | A | Pts |
|--------------|---|---|---|---|---|---|-----|
| Liverpool    | 1 | 1 | 0 | 0 | 6 | 1 | 3   |
| Arsenal      | 1 | 1 | 0 | 0 | 3 | 0 | 3   |
| Newcastle    | 1 | 1 | 0 | 0 | 3 | 1 | 3   |
| Chelsea      | 1 | 1 | 0 | 0 | 2 | 0 | 3   |
| Man Utd      | 1 | 1 | 0 | 0 | 2 | 0 | 3   |
| Tottenham    | 1 | 1 | 0 | 0 | 4 | 3 | 3   |
| Nottm Forest | 1 | 1 | 0 | 0 | 1 | 0 | 3   |
| Aston Villa  | 1 | 0 | 1 | 0 | 2 | 2 | 1   |
| Everton      | 1 | 0 | 1 | 0 | 2 | 2 | 1   |
| Blackburn    | 1 | 0 | 1 | 0 | 1 | 1 | 1   |
| Coventry     | 1 | 0 | 1 | 0 | 1 | 1 | 1   |
| Southampton  | 1 | 0 | 1 | 0 | 1 | 1 | 1   |
| Wimbledon    | 1 | 0 | 1 | 0 | 1 | 1 | 1   |
| Leeds        | 1 | 0 | 1 | 0 | 0 | 0 | 1   |
| West Ham     | 1 | 0 | 1 | 0 | 0 | 0 | 1   |
| Sheff Wed    | 1 | 0 | 0 | 1 | 3 | 4 | 0   |
| Ipswich      | 1 | 0 | 0 | 1 | 0 | 1 | 0   |
| Leicester    | 1 | 0 | 0 | 1 | 1 | 3 | 0   |
| Norwich      | 1 | 0 | 0 | 1 | 0 | 2 | 0   |
| QPR          | 1 | 0 | 0 | 1 | 0 | 2 | 0   |
| Man City     | 1 | 0 | 0 | 1 | 0 | 3 | 0   |
| C Palace     | 1 | 0 | 0 | 1 | 1 | 6 | 0   |

*Andy Cole leaps to beat Richard Smith.*

# *August 24*

---

**NEWCASTLE 4**

COVENTRY 0

*(Half-time score : 3-0)*

*Newcastle:* Srnicek, Venison, Beresford, Fox, Lee, Cole, Sellars (Elliott 75), Hottiger, Peacock, Watson (Mathie 78), Albert.
*Sub:* Hooper.
*Coventry:* Ogrizovic, Borrows, Morgan, Darby, Rennie, Flynn (Pickering 76), Wegerle, Quinn, Jenkinson (Boland 82), Busst, Cook.
*Scorers:* Lee 21, 34, Watson 26, Cole 73.
*Referee:* P Danson (Leicester).
*Attendance:* 34,163

Robert Lee slipped into top gear and drove Newcastle to another scorching win. Lee scored twice as hapless Coventry endured their now customary St James' Park nightmare. Kevin Keegan's high-flyers walloped them 4-0 in the League last season and ushered Phil Neal's side out of the FA Cup as well.

This time the story was much the same with only the goalscorers changing. A delighted Keegan said: "There was some super football, reminiscent of a club we know called Liverpool.

We've come out of the blocks like Linford Christie. Now we've got to go on and show we can finish like Christie as well."

Coventry boss Neal agreed: "Newcastle are realistic title contenders. They remind me of the way Liverpool played when I was there."

Effectively the match was all done and nicely dusted for Newcastle after 35 minutes. That was how long it took them to sweep into a 3-0 lead and impressively follow the 3-1 thrashing of Leicester.

Newcastle have just spent £400,000 on a new pitch and man-of-the-match Lee must have thought it was more of a magic carpet the way he cast a spell over Coventry. Along the way an important question was answered: Newcastle *can* survive without inspirational captain Peter Beardsley who missed this match with a fractured cheekbone.

Lee struck his first goal in the 21st minute and it gave Belgian international Philippe Albert the chance to show he can create as well as destroy. Albert, a £2.65 million signing, played a major role in the build-up. It was developed by Ruel Fox, who shot against Steve Ogrizovic, and Lee pounced to deal with the rebound.

Five minutes later Steve Watson made his own stunning contribution. Darren Peacock and Andy Cole played their parts in winning a Fox corner and Watson beat Ogrizovic with a stupendous shot.

Lee scored his second in the 34th minute, punishing David Rennie for a piece of ineffective defending.

But for a couple of saves from Ogrizovic and a goal-line clearance from Rennie, Newcastle would have been six up at half-time. How could Cole, last season's 41-goal striker, not cash in on such a feast? The night seemed tailor-made for him, yet he missed an easy first-half chance.

He made amends after 73 minutes, however, plundering Newcastle's fourth in cavalier style; and not even the combined efforts of Rennie and his central defensive partner Dave Busst could hold him back. It was tasty fare to set before the occupants of Newcastle's new £8 million exhibition stand.

*League Table After Match*

| | P | W | D | L | F | A | Pts |
|---|---|---|---|---|---|---|---|
| Newcastle | 2 | 2 | 0 | 0 | 7 | 1 | 6 |
| Tottenham | 2 | 2 | 0 | 0 | 6 | 4 | 6 |
| Blackburn | 2 | 1 | 1 | 0 | 4 | 1 | 4 |
| Man Utd | 2 | 1 | 1 | 0 | 3 | 1 | 4 |
| Nottm Forest | 2 | 1 | 1 | 0 | 2 | 1 | 4 |
| Leeds | 2 | 1 | 1 | 0 | 1 | 0 | 4 |
| Liverpool | 1 | 1 | 0 | 0 | 6 | 1 | 3 |
| Arsenal | 2 | 1 | 0 | 1 | 3 | 1 | 3 |
| Chelsea | 1 | 1 | 0 | 0 | 2 | 0 | 3 |
| Man City | 2 | 1 | 0 | 1 | 3 | 3 | 3 |
| QPR | 2 | 1 | 0 | 1 | 3 | 4 | 3 |
| Aston Villa | 2 | 0 | 2 | 0 | 3 | 3 | 2 |
| Southampton | 2 | 0 | 2 | 0 | 2 | 2 | 2 |
| Wimbledon | 2 | 0 | 2 | 0 | 2 | 2 | 2 |
| Everton | 2 | 0 | 1 | 1 | 3 | 4 | 1 |
| Ipswich | 2 | 0 | 1 | 1 | 1 | 2 | 1 |
| Norwich | 2 | 0 | 1 | 1 | 0 | 2 | 1 |
| West Ham | 2 | 0 | 1 | 1 | 0 | 3 | 1 |
| Coventry | 2 | 0 | 1 | 1 | 1 | 5 | 1 |
| C Palace | 2 | 0 | 1 | 1 | 1 | 6 | 1 |
| Sheff Wed | 2 | 0 | 0 | 2 | 4 | 7 | 0 |
| Leicester | 2 | 0 | 0 | 2 | 1 | 6 | 0 |

# *August 27*

---

### NEWCASTLE 5

### SOUTHAMPTON 1

*(Half-time score : 3-0)*

*Newcastle:* Srnicek, Hottiger, Beresford, Venison, Peacock, Albert, Fox (Mathie 60), Watson, Cole, Lee, Sellars (Elliott 79).
*Sub:* Hooper.
*Southampton*: Grobbelaar, Kenna, Benali, Magilton, Hall (Whiston 73), Widdrington (Heaney 45), Le Tissier, Charlton, Banger, Maddison, Allen.
*Scorers:* (Newcastle): Watson 30, 37 Cole 40, 70, Lee 85; (Southampton): Banger 52.
*Referee:* D Elleray (Harrow).
*Attendance:* 34,181

Andy Cole showed once again that he was bang on target for a big season, just like Premiership pack leaders Newcastle: three games, four goals – not bad for reliability and a message that all of Newcastle believes should be heeded by England coach Terry Venables.

Thus far the England chief has shown himself about as keen to get the country's premier marksman to the international starting gate as Alan Sugar is to get Venables back to White Hart Lane for a good old chin-wag. But as way Cole goes on scoring goals – two more in this humbling of Alan Ball's Southampton – how long will Venables be able to resist?

Heads turned towards the directors' box as United's No 9 scored the first of a brace that helped make sure three-in-a-row Newcastle established a pace even champions Manchester United could not match. The look they encountered from Venables was one of inscrutability.

But; if he gave nothing away; neither did Cole, who said: "I knew he was here. I will just keep on playing my football, that's all I can do."

That is all Newcastle have to do to prove themselves worthy title challengers. This may not have been the most rounded performance in their three opening wins but, bearing in mind the chances missed before Robert Lee scored Newcastle's fifth, Cole-created goal, the margin of victory could have been more decisive.

Little wonder Ball talked about being embarrassed to be the Southampton manager. Little wonder Matt le Tissier felt compelled to dummy his way past the Press after a sub-international class performance. No wonder St James' Park is a bingo players' paradise – full houses every week. Ball reminded forthcoming visitors: "They have built a fortress here and it's intimidating."

Saints, whose only goal came from Nick Banger, were intimidated enough to give the game away, mainly through Francis Benali whose nightmare mistakes provided gifts for Cole.

But Steve Watson's two goals were prizes won rather than handed over as he opened the scoring in the 30th minute and added a second seven minutes later.

Despite competition from Watson, Cole, Darren Peacock and the imperious Philippe Albert, the outstanding performer was Barry

Venison. At 30 he gave a stop-start exhibition of the best kind: he was repeatedly the man who stopped Southampton making real inroads and repeatedly the man who got Newcastle started again.

His reading of the game from just in front of the back four was exceptional, As was his use of the ball. Saints overlord Lawrie McMenemy, who sold Venison to Liverpool when he was Sunderland's manager; got a good view of that. He got a good view, too, of Cole and concluded: "He's lethal and has proved himself as good as anyone in the Premiership."

*Andy Cole's flying goal.*

# *August 31*

## WEST HAM 1
## NEWCASTLE 3

*(Half-time score : 0-2)*

*West Ham:* Miklosko, Breacker, Burrows, Potts, Martin, Allen (Jones 75), Butler, Moncur, Holmes, Marsh, Hutchison.
*Newcastle:* Srnicek, Venison, Beresford,Lee (Elliott 59), Cole, Sellars, Hottiger, Mathie, Peacock, Watson, Albert.
*Subs:* Parker, Pilkington, Howey, Hooper.
*Scorers:* (West Ham): Hutchison 87 pen; (Newcastle): Potts 32 og, Lee 35, Mathie 88.
*Referee:* B Hill (Leicester).
*Attendance:* 18,580

Newcastle powered back to the top of the Premiership with another cultured display. Kevin Keegan's side have begun with four straight wins, reminiscent of the way they won promotion two seasons ago when they started with 10.

Certainly the army of Geordie fans in London believed they were witnessing something special. The only blemish was the ankle injury which forced Robert Lee out of the action, making him doubtful for England's date with the United States at Wembley.

At the heart of the performance, inevitably, was Andy Cole, though this time as goal maker. The phenomenal striker; who cannot make the England set-up, has scored so many goals for Newcastle in the past 18 months that it is easy to forget he can also create.

He proved his all-round worth to the side in a superb five-minute spell in the first half as Newcastle took command. First he squirmed clear of veteran Alvin Martin inside the box to reach the by-line. Cole's intention was to find striking partner Steve Watson but the cross deflected into goal off the unlucky Hammers' captain Steve Potts.

In the 35th minute Cole's contribution was even more measured. He drifted wide to the left wing to provide an outlet for a sparkling move from defence engineered by Barry Venison and John Beresford. Looking up, Cole spotted Lee's darting run into the West Ham penalty area and threaded a fabulous pass for the new England squad member to steer past the stranded goalkeeper Ludo Miklosko.

Newcastle, despite the absence of injury victims Peter Beardsley and Ruel Fox, were in irresistible mood again. Lee had darted cleverly into the box in the 19th minute but his skimming cross just evaded Cole's outstretched leg.

While Newcastle have begun the season at an average of four goals a game, West Ham went into the match as the only Premiership side yet to score. It was easy to see why. Even the presence of £1.5 million record signing Don Hutchison in attack failed to spark the home side. The former Liverpool player, a Geordie fanatic on the Gallowgate terrace in his youth, did have one volley on target but it was straight at Pavel Srnicek.

West Ham finally scored the goal their brave late rally deserved when Hutchison stroked home an 87th-minute penalty after Beresford had handled. But Newcastle immediately restored their two-goal advantage through Alex Mathie, set up by another Cole run down the right.

Keegan said: "We are giving the first goal to Cole. It was his shot that did the damage. I told him he must keep knocking on the England door."

West Ham manager Harry Redknapp was pleased with the way his players responded to the fierce Newcastle challenge. "People can think what they like about us but we know we'll do OK. We played well tonight. We're not far from being a decent side."

### League Table After Match

| | P | W | D | L | F | A | Pts |
|---|---|---|---|---|---|---|---|
| Newcastle | 4 | 4 | 0 | 0 | 15 | 3 | 12 |
| Man Utd | 4 | 3 | 1 | 0 | 7 | 1 | 10 |
| Nottm Forest | 4 | 3 | 1 | 0 | 5 | 2 | 10 |
| Liverpool | 3 | 3 | 0 | 0 | 11 | 1 | 9 |
| Chelsea | 3 | 3 | 0 | 0 | 8 | 2 | 9 |
| Tottenham | 4 | 3 | 0 | 1 | 9 | 6 | 9 |
| Blackburn | 4 | 2 | 2 | 0 | 8 | 1 | 8 |
| Leeds | 4 | 2 | 1 | 1 | 5 | 4 | 7 |
| Man City | 4 | 2 | 0 | 2 | 7 | 6 | 6 |
| Aston Villa | 4 | 1 | 3 | 0 | 5 | 4 | 6 |
| Norwich | 4 | 1 | 2 | 1 | 1 | 2 | 5 |
| Sheff Wed | 4 | 1 | 1 | 2 | 6 | 7 | 4 |
| Arsenal | 4 | 1 | 1 | 2 | 3 | 4 | 4 |
| QPR | 4 | 1 | 1 | 2 | 5 | 7 | 4 |
| Ipswich | 4 | 1 | 1 | 2 | 4 | 6 | 4 |
| Wimbledon | 4 | 0 | 2 | 2 | 2 | 6 | 2 |
| C Palace | 4 | 0 | 2 | 2 | 3 | 9 | 2 |
| Southampton | 4 | 0 | 2 | 2 | 3 | 9 | 2 |
| Everton | 4 | 0 | 1 | 3 | 4 | 10 | 1 |
| Leicester | 4 | 0 | 1 | 3 | 2 | 8 | 1 |
| West Ham | 4 | 0 | 1 | 3 | 2 | 8 | 1 |
| Coventry | 4 | 0 | 1 | 3 | 1 | 10 | 1 |

# *September 10*

---

**NEWCASTLE 4**

**CHELSEA 2**

*(Half-time score : 2-2)*

*Newcastle:* Hooper, Hottiger, Beresford, Venison, Peacock, Albert, Fox, Lee, Cole, Watson, Sellars.
*Subs:* Howey, Mathie, Burridge.
*Chelsea:* Kharine, Clarke, Spackman (Newton 74), Kjeldbjerg, Johnsen, Sinclair, Spencer, Peacock, Furlong, Wise, Rocastle (Hoddle 76).
*Scorers:* (Newcastle): Cole 7, 66, Fox 21, Lee 53; (Chelsea): Peacock 15, Furlong 27.
*Referee:* P Jones (Loughborough).
*Attendance:* 34,435

---

Kevin Keegan and Glenn Hoddle are the missionaries of modern football, spreading the word that their sport can be greatly improved when the yokes of fear and caution are lifted from the shoulders of their players.

Their own lives have long been secured by the riches they earned with their feet, so the gospel they preach is not inhibited by the threat that failure might cost anything more than a loss of pride.

This was as much a carnival as a football match in which two of the game's brightest and most talented managers had decided, without exchanging a word, that their teams would further enrich a season already throbbing with entertainment.

Keegan, looking down from the mountain his team sits astride, would be the first to acknowledge the part Chelsea played in an exhilarating match. It was a game that had everything but sound defending; where the commitment to attack was so great that something had to give and where one young man's reputation, already on a upward spiral, was propelled higher by a goal of awesome power.

Andy Cole represents the traditions of Newcastle, a club where great centre-forwards have been revered. But even cherished predecessors Jackie Milburn and Malcolm MacDonald would have acclaimed the goal that set this game on its mesmerising course. It was struck, left-footed, from the left hand edge of the area and exploded on its target with the force of a cannon shell, just beneath the near - post angle where crossbar meets upright.

An admiring Keegan said: "You can always tell when an exceptional goal is scored because you get a split-second of drawn breath before the cheers, as if the fans are saying 'Did that really happen?' It was a classic goal."

But there was much more to this match than the frightening potential of Cole. There was the wizardry of Ruel Fox, playing in the Peter Beardsley role, the powerful precociousness of Steve Watson and the galloping charges of Philippe Albert.

And that was just Newcastle. Chelsea provided the acrobatic goalkeeping of Dmitri Kharine, the orchestration of Gavin Peacock, the aggressive drive of Dennis Wise and the agility of Paul Furlong.

"We came up here with no fear," said a disappointed Hoddle. "We matched them for creation and passing. They always looked as if they would score goals. And so did we.

"Chelsea have come a long way in 12 months, so it is not all doom and gloom for us. There was a lot of good movement and at times we opened up their defence for fun. But they open you up at the other end."

Chelsea have indeed advanced, and refreshingly so, but if they have moved forward like an InterCity 125, then Newcastle's progress under Keegan has been more a flight on Concorde.

Keegan admitted, that Newcastle were a bit kamikaze at times. But this was not the day to criticise his gung-ho defenders. "I have encouraged that attitude, so it's partly my fault," he said.

"I have told Albert and the full-backs to get forward, so I can't cry when other teams exploit that weakness if we don't then use the ball properly. Anyway it has won us five games out of five.

"If we have the ball, we look to attack teams. The trouble is, when we have not got it we are supposed to defend better than we did today. But we have taken part in a great game and won 4-2."

Keegan has ever been a patriot but there does seem merit in his claim that we are offering the world the finest league to be found anywhere this season. "If there is a better one, then I'd like to watch it," he said. "Look at all the players who have been brought in during the past 12 months. I don't think even the Italian League can be better at present."

Certainly no European nation offers more fervour among fans than was demonstrated on Tyneside. "The expectation is enormous," said Keegan, "and the players are aware of it.

"When I came here some players would sneak in through the back door. Now they stick their chests out and walk through the front because they are all players with ability. I don't want to be unkind to some of the others but the club was too big for them."

Cole, of course, is their catalyst and it is inevitable that sooner or later his talent will force him on to the international stage. But Keegan will not rush him. "He is doing it the right way," he said. "He hasn't gone into print saying he should be getting chosen for this or that. He

*Andy Cole celebrates his wonder goal.*

is saying: 'Yes, there are a lot of good strikers around but I am going to keep scoring goals, keep knocking on the door because eventually, if you knock enough, someone opens it'.

"What he does out there is what he lives for. He just wants to score goals. But what has really pleased me this year is the way he has got hold of the ball and shielded it.

"He will always get goals because he has pace and is a good finisher. It is the other parts he needs to acquire to keep on advancing. But you say something to him and it's as if it has been filed on computer. This season he has played with four different partners up front and he has looked a class act with every one of them. You have to give him credit for adapting so well."

When Newcastle went 4-2 ahead Keegan looked around at the fans in their black-and-white shirts. "We aren't half making up for lost time," he said. "The fans had a bleak period when they didn't have much to shout about. Now we are building real memories for them."

### League Table After Match

|              | P | W | D | L | F  | A  | Pts |
|--------------|---|---|---|---|----|----|-----|
| Newcastle    | 5 | 5 | 0 | 0 | 19 | 5  | 15  |
| Nottm Forest | 5 | 4 | 1 | 0 | 9  | 3  | 13  |
| Blackburn    | 5 | 3 | 2 | 0 | 11 | 1  | 11  |
| Liverpool    | 4 | 3 | 1 | 0 | 11 | 1  | 10  |
| Man Utd      | 5 | 3 | 1 | 1 | 8  | 3  | 10  |
| Leeds        | 5 | 3 | 1 | 1 | 7  | 5  | 10  |
| Chelsea      | 4 | 3 | 0 | 1 | 10 | 6  | 9   |
| Tottenham    | 4 | 3 | 0 | 1 | 9  | 6  | 9   |
| Aston Villa  | 5 | 2 | 3 | 0 | 7  | 4  | 9   |
| Man City     | 5 | 2 | 1 | 2 | 8  | 7  | 7   |
| Norwich      | 5 | 1 | 3 | 1 | 1  | 2  | 6   |
| Arsenal      | 5 | 1 | 2 | 2 | 3  | 4  | 5   |
| QPR          | 5 | 1 | 2 | 2 | 7  | 9  | 5   |
| Wimbledon    | 5 | 1 | 2 | 2 | 4  | 7  | 5   |
| Sheff Wed    | 5 | 1 | 1 | 3 | 7  | 11 | 4   |
| Ipswich      | 5 | 1 | 1 | 3 | 4  | 8  | 4   |
| C Palace     | 5 | 0 | 3 | 2 | 4  | 10 | 3   |
| Southampton  | 4 | 0 | 2 | 2 | 3  | 9  | 2   |
| West Ham     | 5 | 0 | 2 | 3 | 1  | 7  | 2   |
| Coventry     | 5 | 0 | 2 | 3 | 3  | 12 | 2   |
| Leicester    | 5 | 0 | 1 | 4 | 3  | 10 | 1   |
| Everton      | 5 | 0 | 1 | 4 | 4  | 13 | 1   |

# *September 13*

---

Kevin Keegan saluted his Newcastle side as better than Liverpool following their sizzling European return.

The Geordies, led by Robert Lee's hat-trick of headers, hammered Royal Antwerp in the first leg of their Uefa Cup first-round tie. And Keegan proclaimed: "Bearing in mind this was our first time in Europe it was brilliant. That performance was as incredible as any I've seen. Even Liverpool didn't play like that away from home."

In turn chairman Sir John Hall, whose dream it is to make Newcastle kings of Europe, saluted Keegan and his Euro stars. "I am sitting here trying to believe that it has all happened," he said. "We have seen the very best of British football tonight – and long may it continue."

Lee made an astounding contribution to a high-quality United performance. It allowed Keegan's side, operating at this level for the first time in 17 years, to set out their Uefa Cup credentials in the most authoritative manner. Long before it was over, Antwerp were made to feel second-raters, an unfamiliar sensation for a team who reached the final of the Cup Winners' Cup in 1993, beaten at Wembley by Parma.

Newcastle played all the right cards at all the right times and, with the game won, Keegan played another midway through the second half. Andy Cole got himself booked for a foul on Manuel Godfroid and, with tempers set to flare, was immediately substituted.

United's Belgian defender Philippe Albert had predicted United were capable of grabbing vital away goals but no one could have forecast they would arrive so quickly. There were 52 seconds on the clock when Lee claimed his spectacular first, a brave diving header as he flicked John Beresford's cross beyond Antwerp keeper Ratko Svilar. It was a superb piece of finishing from the 28-year-old midfield player, recently recruited to Terry Venables' international set.

And such was his desire to leave a scorching impression on the game that he grabbed another after eight minutes. He started the move himself, Ruel Fox crossed to the six-yard line and Lee tore in and beat not only two home defenders to the ball but also Cole. It silenced the home fans and brought United's band to the boil.

Keegan's only concern in the opening half was the fitness of goal-

---

**ROYAL ANTWERP 0**

**NEWCASTLE 5**

*(Half-time score : 0-3)*

*Antwerp:* Svilar, Vangompel, Broeckaert, Kulcsar, Smidts, Emmerechts, Kiekens, Porter, Severeyns, Zohar (Monteiro 67), Godfroid.
*Newcastle:* Srnicek, Hottiger, Beresford, Venison, Fox, Albert, Lee, Beardsley (Watson 69), Cole (Jeffrey 69), Peacock, Sellars.
*Sub:* Hooper.
*Scorers:* Lee 1, 9, 51, Sellars 40, Watson 78.
*Referee:* R Wojcik (Poland).
*Attendance:* 15,000

keeper Pavel Srnicek after a collision with Antwerp's top scorer Francis Seveneyns, whose pace took him onto Albert's headed back-pass, but the keeper continued after treatment.

As promised, Keegan went ahead with his plan to push Peter Beardsley back into action three weeks ahead of schedule. But, instead of getting his taste of European soccer alongside Cole, Beardsley played on the right of midfield.

United's third came after Antwerp had done their unconvincing best to repair Lee's damage, and the strike underlined Cole's goal-making qualities. He won a Fox cross and teed it up for Scott Sellars to slot in his first goal of the season.

Lee produced another piece of lethal finishing to complete his hat-trick six minutes into the second half. Again it was a header, nodding Marc Hottiger's cleverly cut-back cross past a sickened Svilar.

Amid it all the Belgians did create scoring opportunities; only a super save from Srnicek stopped Seveneyns getting them back in the game. But substitute Steve Watson wriggled his way past three defenders to make it 5-0 after 78 minutes.

*Robert Lee heads the second.*

# September 18

Peter Beardsley, the Peter Pan of English football, added another colourful chapter to Newcastle's fairy-tale start to the season at a captivated Highbury. Arsenal, whose defence was once the meanest in the Premiership, looked as if they had been trapped in a revolving door as United made it 22 goals in six straight victories.

That is a record for Newcastle at the game's top level and no less than their uninhibited football warranted. George Graham's men may feel aggrieved that they got nothing for prolonged possession in the Newcastle half and look ruefully at a league table that sees them already 13 points adrift of the leaders.

But Newcastle are harvesting a rich crop from their commitment to attack and, whoever you support, they are the most colourful side in the Premiership this season.

The return of Beardsley up front enhanced their attacking philosophy and he was at the centre of this stunning victory in his 500th league game. With Barry Venison absent, Kevin Keegan played an extra centre-half but it made little difference to Newcastle's drive, merely encouraging Philippe Albert and the full-backs to go forward more often.

Andy Cole, back at Highbury where it all began for him, let nostalgia dull his usual threat. Perhaps facing Tony Adams, whose boots he used to polish, led him to show too much respect but there are so many cylinders to Newcastle's engine that it still roared throatily.

With Arsenal playing penetrative passing football we once again had a match that bristled and sparkled, the tempo rarely dropping below quick-step and the goalkeepers showing off their athleticism.

Pavel Srnicek did so in the sixth minute with an upstretched hand to deny Paul Merson, enjoying one of his most impressive and busy matches for some time. It was a crucial save. A minute later United were in front. Martin Keown headed out a Marc Hottiger cross and Beardsley drove back a shot which deflected off Keown past David Seaman going the other way.

That lead was quickly obliterated when Merson's free-kick flew up off the wall and Adams, at the second attempt, got it over the line for Arsenal's first Premiership goal in almost six-and-a-half hours.

---

**ARSENAL 2**

**NEWCASTLE 3**

*(Half-time score : 1-2)*

*Arsenal:* Seaman, Dixon, Winterburn, Jensen (Selley 70), Keown, Adams, Parlour (Campbell 70), Wright, Smith, Merson, Schwarz.
*Newcastle:* Srnicek, Hottiger, Beresford, Howey, Peacock, Albert, Lee, Beardsley, Cole, Fox, Sellars.
*Subs:* Watson, Mathie, Hooper.
*Scorers:* (Arsenal): Adams 9, Wright 88; (Newcastle): Beardsley 7, 45 pen, Fox 74.
*Referee:* T Holbrook (Walsall).
*Attendance:* 36,819

---

Srnicek denied Merson's clever flick and Alan Smith drove just too high as Arsenal seemed set to take over. But when Albert strode forward to meet Ruel Fox's cross Lee Dixon pushed him in the back and Beardsley does not miss too many from the penalty spot.

The entertainment did not dip in the second half. Merson twice threatened with far-post headers, but as Arsenal plunged forward for the equaliser, there were gaps at the back. Nobody exploits space better than Beardsley and in the 75th minute his shot hit Dixon and rebounded to Fox. From a narrow angle he drove it against the underside of the bar and, as it came down, it hit Keown and went in.

Newcastle were in control and not even Ian Wright's 89th-minute goal from the edge of the area and off the inside of a post could detract from Beardsley's day.

Afterwards Arsenal manager George Graham backed Newcastle to win the Premiership. "They are championship material," said Graham, who has steered Arsenal to two titles. "They might be vulnerable defensively but going forward they are excellent. They have been a

*Peter Beardsley and Andy Cole celebrate victory over Arsenal.*

breath of fresh air. They are exciting to watch and they bring out the best in other people.

"They were a little fortunate today because until the last 20 minutes we were the better team. We gave them a leg-up with a big deflection and a penalty for the first two goals. But after their third they were superb. They really started to blossom."

For the first time in two years Manchester United, at 7-4, have been replaced as title favourites by Newcastle, quoted at 13-8.

Keegan was full of praise for Beardsley. "He is a gem to have around the club. He is building a house in the North-East and we are going to put a big fence around it to keep him there," he said.

He admitted that Arsenal were a little unfortunate. "On the balance of play they probably deserved to get something out of the game. But the team that takes the chances wins," he said.

"That was a severe test for us because Arsenal were excellent. We were under the cosh. But if you want to stay top of the league and the football isn't flowing, you have to battle."

### League Table After Match

|              | P | W | D | L | F  | A  | Pts |
|--------------|---|---|---|---|----|----|-----|
| Newcastle    | 6 | 6 | 0 | 0 | 22 | 7  | 18  |
| Blackburn    | 6 | 4 | 2 | 0 | 13 | 2  | 14  |
| Nottm Forest | 6 | 4 | 2 | 0 | 10 | 4  | 14  |
| Man Utd      | 6 | 4 | 1 | 1 | 10 | 3  | 13  |
| Liverpool    | 5 | 3 | 1 | 1 | 11 | 3  | 10  |
| Leeds        | 6 | 3 | 1 | 2 | 8  | 7  | 10  |
| Chelsea      | 5 | 3 | 0 | 2 | 11 | 8  | 9   |
| Aston Villa  | 6 | 2 | 3 | 1 | 2  | 5  | 9   |
| Tottenham    | 6 | 3 | 0 | 3 | 11 | 11 | 9   |
| Norwich      | 6 | 2 | 3 | 1 | 3  | 3  | 9   |
| Man City     | 6 | 2 | 2 | 2 | 9  | 8  | 8   |
| QPR          | 6 | 1 | 3 | 2 | 9  | 11 | 6   |
| Wimbledon    | 6 | 1 | 3 | 2 | 4  | 7  | 6   |
| Southampton  | 6 | 1 | 3 | 2 | 6  | 11 | 6   |
| Arsenal      | 6 | 1 | 2 | 3 | 5  | 7  | 5   |
| Sheff Wed    | 6 | 1 | 2 | 3 | 8  | 12 | 5   |
| West Ham     | 6 | 1 | 2 | 3 | 2  | 7  | 5   |
| Coventry     | 6 | 1 | 2 | 3 | 5  | 13 | 5   |
| Leicester    | 6 | 1 | 1 | 4 | 6  | 11 | 4   |
| Ipswich      | 6 | 1 | 1 | 4 | 5  | 10 | 4   |
| C Palace     | 6 | 0 | 4 | 2 | 4  | 10 | 4   |
| Everton      | 6 | 0 | 2 | 4 | 6  | 15 | 2   |

# September 21

## NEWCASTLE 2
## BARNSLEY 1
*(Half-time score : 1-1)*

*Newcastle:* Srnicek, Hottiger, Beresford, Peacock, Howey, Albert (Mathie 90), Lee, Beardsley, Sellars (Watson 69), Fox, Cole.
*Sub:* Hooper.
*Barnsley:* Watson, Bishop, Fleming, Taggart, Davis, Snodin, Wilson, O'Connell, Redfearn, Rammell (Liddell 90), Payton.
*Scorers:* (Newcastle): Cole 25, Fox 85; (Barnsley): Redfearn 20.
*Referee:* R A Hart (Darlington).
*Attendance:* 27,208

*Andy Cole celebrates his goal.*

Ruel Fox rescued Newcastle when they were five minutes away from losing their 100 per cent record.

Newcastle have swept all before them in the Premiership and the Uefa Cup this season, yet almost came unstuck in the Coca-Cola Cup first leg against battling Barnsley from the First Division.

Barnsley were in control for long periods and in sight of a proud draw until Fox struck. The winger moved in at the near post to turn in a low right-wing cross from substitute Steve Watson.

The relief within St James' Park was equalled by Fox's as he saw the ball go past impressive young keeper David Watson. Eleven minutes earlier Fox had wasted a glorious opportunity on a rare occasion when Newcastle found a way through Barnsley's sweeper system.

It seemed that Fox's blunder, after a brilliant reverse pass by Robert Lee, would cost them their chance of taking a lead to Oakwell for the second leg.

Barnsley certainly deserved to be level. Their passing and movement were even better than Newcastle's as United suffered their first off-day of the season. Barnsley even had the cheek to take the lead in the 20th minute. Neil Redfearn, at his eighth club, was the scorer with a spectacular 25-yard effort at the end of a typically patient build-up.

Andy Cole, subdued by Barnsley's defence for most of the night, hit back with a close-range header after being set up by John Beresford and Fox in the 25th minute.

Barnsley boss Danny Wilson was rightly disappointed. "People thought we were here to make up the numbers," he said. "Now they know different."

# September 24

Terry Venables popped into a Newcastle bookshop, signed a few copies of his latest literary work and moved on to St James' Park. Then Venables headed off home, maybe to write a new chapter into the footballing life of Steve McManaman.

Despite huge natural talent, McManaman lost his way last season which may not be too surprising considering the signs of confusion posted around Anfield. But on a day when Liverpool became the first Premiership side this season to stop Newcastle knocking out a win the message was clear: he has clearly found himself.

If McManaman keeps on playing with the same sort of verve, he could well find himself being ushered into the England team. He scared the life out of Newcastle.

Frightening was the word Neil Ruddock used to describe the level of form the 22-year-old Liverpudlian is exhibiting. "I'd say he deserves his chance," declared the Anfield defender.

Venables might agree but what will he think of the crop of Newcastle players who have clamoured for his attention during a hitherto flawless start to the campaign and largely missed this chance to push their claims? The England coach may not be able to get a seat at White Hart Lane these days but it looks as though he is going to make the North-East his second home.

This was his second visit to the House of Keegan inside a few weeks. And if there were flashes of excitement there were dollops of disappointment too. Half the time Newcastle did not look like Newcastle, certainly not the team who have had the bookies revising the title odds.

Even Keegan could scarcely believe their feeble first-half offering. He called them "chocolate men" at half-time because of the way they melted away in challenge after challenge.

"You may laugh at that but that's what I saw," said Keegan. "Every time we went into a tackle Liverpool came out with the ball and that's not like us. I said we had to start getting the ball before we could even think about anything tactical. Every time a ball bounced 50-50 they came away with it."

That made it all the more surprising Newcastle scored first, a beauty

---

**NEWCASTLE 1**

**LIVERPOOL 1**

*(Half-time score : 0-0)*

*Newcastle:* Srnicek, Hottiger, Beresford, Venison (Howey 23), Peacock, Albert, Lee, Beardsley, Sellars (Watson 83), Fox, Cole. *Sub:* Hooper.
*Liverpool:* James, Jones, Scales, Ruddock, Bjornebye, Babb, McManaman, Fowler, Molby, Rush (Clough 90), Barnes.
*Scorers:* (Newcastle): Lee 50; (Liverpool): Rush 70.
*Referee:* P Don (Middlesex).
*Attendance:* 34,435

---

out of nothing from Robert Lee and his ninth of the season. Only then did Newcastle show a more appealing profile. But this is a Liverpool team better than anything seen for some time – not the old Liverpool but very possibly the new.

There was lots of good passing and lots of inventive movement, with the newly instituted back three of John Scales, Ruddock and Phil Babb performing in unison. McManaman hit the bar, post and heights of exhilarating excellence; John Barnes and Jan Molby were tremendous midfield influences.

Keegan normally likes to sing the praises of his own team but sportingly sang for Liverpool when he said: "They are a very experienced side. And they are also a bit of a wounded animal. People have written them off, they have said the club is not what it used to be. Well, you know how dangerous wounded animals can be. They can have a say in the championship."

Liverpool, who may not get the ball in the box as often as they ought, claimed the point they deserved when skipper Ian Rush produced a 25-yarder that made the otherwise in-form Pavel Srnicek look out of touch.

But in view of the season the goalkeeper is having it would be harsh to be too critical and the same could go for his team-mates who were out-passed in the first half. Remember, they are still two points clear at the top.

But they will miss Barry Venison, who faces a month on the sidelines with a torn hamstring, while Philippe Albert faces suspension following his late sending-off.

Maybe it is as well Paul Kitson changed his mind about not joining Keegan and returned to his native North-East to sign for £2.25m on Saturday.

## *League Table After Match*

| | P | W | D | L | F | A | Pts |
|---|---|---|---|---|---|---|---|
| Newcastle | 7 | 6 | 1 | 0 | 23 | 8 | 19 |
| Blackburn | 7 | 5 | 2 | 0 | 16 | 3 | 17 |
| Nottm Forest | 7 | 5 | 2 | 0 | 14 | 5 | 17 |
| Man Utd | 7 | 4 | 1 | 2 | 12 | 6 | 13 |
| Chelsea | 6 | 4 | 0 | 2 | 12 | 8 | 12 |
| Liverpool | 6 | 3 | 2 | 1 | 12 | 4 | 11 |
| Man City | 7 | 3 | 2 | 2 | 11 | 8 | 11 |
| Leeds | 6 | 3 | 1 | 2 | 8 | 7 | 10 |
| Aston Villa | 7 | 2 | 3 | 2 | 8 | 8 | 9 |
| Wimbledon | 7 | 2 | 3 | 2 | 5 | 7 | 9 |
| Norwich | 7 | 2 | 3 | 2 | 3 | 5 | 9 |
| Tottenham | 7 | 3 | 0 | 4 | 12 | 15 | 9 |
| Southampton | 7 | 2 | 3 | 2 | 9 | 12 | 9 |
| Arsenal | 7 | 2 | 2 | 3 | 7 | 7 | 8 |
| Ipswich | 7 | 2 | 1 | 4 | 8 | 12 | 7 |
| QPR | 7 | 1 | 3 | 3 | 9 | 12 | 6 |
| Sheff Wed | 6 | 1 | 2 | 3 | 8 | 12 | 5 |
| Leicester | 7 | 1 | 2 | 4 | 7 | 12 | 5 |
| West Ham | 7 | 1 | 2 | 4 | 2 | 9 | 5 |
| Coventry | 7 | 1 | 2 | 4 | 6 | 16 | 5 |
| C Palace | 7 | 0 | 4 | 3 | 4 | 11 | 4 |
| Everton | 7 | 0 | 3 | 4 | 7 | 16 | 3 |

# September 27

Newcastle completed their Belgian demolition job in the style one would expect from prospective conquerors of Europe. Instead of sitting back on their five-goal lead they built on it, inspired by an Andy Cole hat-trick, to give Antwerp their second hiding in a fortnight.

This was the first time Newcastle had staged front-line European football for 17 years and United boss Kevin Keegan had vowed to put on a show worthy of the occasion. His Uefa Cup first-footers did exactly that by blitzing the Belgians with four goals in a rousing opening half.

It means Newcastle go into Friday's second-round draw as the side even top European outfits would prefer to avoid. Keegan said: "We are on an adventure, and the adventure continues. It was a great performance."

Antwerp had changed their goalkeeper from the first leg in a bid to bring them better defensive luck. But, just as Ratko Svilar had been overwhelmed in Belgium, so was his replacement Yves Van Der Straeten.

There were only 11 minutes on the clock when Robert Lee, the first-leg hat-trick hero, took his tally over the two legs to four, and 10 for the season. Antwerp skipper Rudi Smidts failed to get enough distance on a clearance from Ruel Fox's corner and Lee, just outside the area, reacted quickly to lob the ball back into the net.

Despite Newcastle's unassailable position, Keegan had shown Antwerp and his own fans every respect by turning out a full-strength side. That included Cole, whom the United boss had been tempted to rest because of shin problems.

Cole was clearly desperate to collect his first European goal and he got it after 26 minutes. It was possibly the easiest he will claim all season. Scott Sellars did the hard bit, springing Antwerp's faulty off-side trap courtesy of a ball from Fox, and then cut his cross back so well that Cole was left with the job of walking in his eighth goal of the season.

Philippe Albert, who was operating as a midfield anchorman, seemed just as keen as Cole to be a part of Newcastle's goal splurge.

## NEWCASTLE 5
## ROYAL ANTWERP 2
*(Half-time score : 4-0*
*Agg. score: 10-2)*

*Newcastle:* Srnicek, Hottiger, Beresford, Peacock, Albert, Howey, Fox, Lee (Watson 72), Beardsley (Clark 46), Cole, Sellars.
*Antwerp:* Van Der Straeten, Vangompel (Moukrim 87), Taeymans, Kulcsar, Smidts, Emmerechts (Monteiro 45), Kiekens, Porte, Severeyns, Zohar, Godfroid.
*Scorers:* (Newcastle): Lee 11, Cole 26, 39, 88, Beardsley 36 pen; (Royal Antwerp): Kiekens 75, Severeyns 77.
*Referee:* R Pederson (Norway).
*Attendance:* 29,737

Twice he produced finger-burning examples of power shooting to frighten the life out of Van Der Straeten.

The third goal arrived after 36 minutes. Fox earned a penalty when he was brought down by Manuel Godfroid and Peter Beardsley had the pleasure of scoring. Then the United captain set up the fourth for Cole three minutes later.

Newcastle fans did not mind giving the Belgians two of the biggest cheers of the night when they got cheeky and scored twice. Wim Kiekens beat Pavel Srnicek with a diving header and Francis Seveneyns fired home a superb shot.

Cole completed his hat-trick two minutes from time after Sellars' jinking run.

*Robert Lee scores*
*Newcastle's first*
*in the 11th minute.*

# October 1

Ron Atkinson believes he could be looking at the future champions of England when he puts on the video of Newcastle's latest victory. But he will be looking for clues as well, evidence of the robbery committed at Villa Park.

"Can you understand that?" Atkinson asked after Newcastle's win. "How can my players feel about that? They've played so well – more than well enough to win – and they've got nothing."

Villa were the victims of a Newcastle team that lived off the confidence built during their stunning start to the season. Everything, including goals, went against them.

"Newcastle have enough points in the bag now to have an excellent chance of staying the pace in the championship race," said Atkinson. "I have no argument with them on that but, let's be honest, they shouldn't have won here, should they?"

Villa continued where they left off against Inter Milan, pounding away at Newcastle but unable to score a goal to save their lives. Or, as Andy Townsend put it after one of his best games for Villa: "The ball just wouldn't go over the dammed line."

On the other hand Newcastle, as effusive as Danny Baker when they get into their stride, are always likely to get a goal, and that is exactly what happened. When Nigel Spink and Paul McGrath made their late mistakes, the game was over, won for Newcastle by Robert Lee and Andy Cole.

"While Newcastle have goal-scorers like that in their line-up, then they are going to get goals and that, with the quality of their football, makes them genuine title material," says Atkinson.

Villa could hardly believe the slap in the face they took. "That might be as well as we have played in two years," added the Villa manager. "And yet we have finished beaten because we didn't take our chances. We didn't put them away, they did. End of story."

Villa's opportunity to become the first side to beat Newcastle this season came and went in the first half. "We knew we were poor when we came off and the manager made sure we knew it at half-time," said Peter Beardsley.

"It doesn't happen often that we drop below our standards but,

## ASTON VILLA 0
## NEWCASTLE 2
*(Half-time score : 0-0)*

*Villa:* Spink, Barrett, King, Ehiogu, McGrath, Parker, Houghton (Staunton 79), Townsend, Yorke, Fenton (Lamptey 73), Whittingham.
*Newcastle:* Srnicek, Howey, Beresford, Peacock, Albert, Hottiger, Fox, Lee, Beardsley (Kitson 76), Cole, Sellars.
*Subs:* Watson, Hooper.
*Scorers:* Lee 66, Cole 83.
*Referee:* D Gallagher (Banbury).
*Attendance:* 29,960

when it does, Kevin Keegan makes his point very forcibly. And he was entitled to on Saturday. This was an occasion when we needed a kick up the backside and he's not afraid to give it."

Keegan's No 2 Terry McDermott described the one-sided conversation as "paint being stripped off the walls" because, as Beardsley said, Newcastle could have been three down and the game over before KK had time to get a word in.

"The thing about Kevin Keegan is that he comes over as this nice guy and most of the time he is just that," added Darren Peacock, who was so busy in the first 45 minutes he must have been dizzy with the pace and variety of Villa's football.

"But when he's angry and feels we are letting ourselves down, he lets you know it. He doesn't send tea-cups flying, he just tells you what's wrong, the lessons you have forgotten, and reminds you of what's made you into a good side in the first place."

Peacock added: "And he preaches attacking football. The best way to get a home crowd quiet, he says, is to get a couple of goals. There's none of these shutting-up-shop tactics. Wherever we go, whatever happens this season, you can bet that we'll go to grounds to attack and score goals.

"We don't feel invincible but we do feel that Newcastle can go to any ground in the country and attack, score goals and win."

It was that belief that carried Newcastle through a torrid first half where Villa looked at them and saw only the stripes of Inter Milan, picking up their football from where they had left off in last Thursday's epic.

If Villa lacked any power in their legs at all, it was when they came to shooting. Guy Whittingham is about as lucky as Jack Duckworth is industrious. Nothing he did against Inter brought him a goal and it was the same here. Graham Fenton had the worst game of his young career and when Townsend tried to help out the second-string attack, he too, met only frustration.

McDermott revealed: "Our manager had a few words. He was scathing – as fired up as I have seen him and he came out with a few home truths. The goalkeeper kept us in the game up until half-time, and he was the only one to escape when Kevin got stuck in to them.

"Their reaction was that second-half performance and we've finished up with points when we haven't played well."

Sound familiar? Did not Liverpool do that in their glory days? McDermott remembers it that way.

"I played in a lot of title-winning sides at Liverpool and what we are achieving now is very similar to what we experienced at Liverpool," he said. "I don't think anyone will be able to achieve the domination they had for 20 years but we have the same kind of hallmark."

Atkinson suffered then, his Manchester United side missing out on titles because of Liverpool, and now he can see the bonny lads rising as their successors.

### League Table After Match

| | P | W | D | L | F | A | Pts |
|---|---|---|---|---|---|---|---|
| Newcastle | 8 | 7 | 1 | 0 | 25 | 8 | 22 |
| Nottm Forest | 8 | 6 | 2 | 0 | 17 | 7 | 20 |
| Blackburn | 8 | 5 | 2 | 1 | 17 | 5 | 17 |
| Man Utd | 8 | 5 | 1 | 2 | 14 | 6 | 16 |
| Liverpool | 7 | 4 | 2 | 1 | 16 | 5 | 14 |
| Leeds | 8 | 4 | 2 | 2 | 11 | 8 | 14 |
| Chelsea | 7 | 4 | 0 | 3 | 13 | 10 | 12 |
| Southampton | 8 | 3 | 3 | 2 | 12 | 13 | 12 |
| Norwich | 8 | 3 | 3 | 2 | 5 | 6 | 12 |
| Tottenham | 8 | 4 | 0 | 4 | 14 | 16 | 12 |
| Man City | 8 | 3 | 2 | 3 | 11 | 10 | 11 |
| Aston Villa | 8 | 2 | 3 | 3 | 8 | 10 | 9 |
| Wimbledon | 8 | 2 | 3 | 3 | 6 | 9 | 9 |
| Arsenal | 8 | 2 | 2 | 4 | 8 | 9 | 8 |
| West Ham | 8 | 2 | 2 | 4 | 4 | 10 | 8 |
| Ipswich | 8 | 2 | 1 | 5 | 9 | 15 | 7 |
| C Palace | 8 | 1 | 4 | 3 | 6 | 12 | 7 |
| QPR | 8 | 1 | 3 | 4 | 11 | 15 | 6 |
| Sheff Wed | 8 | 1 | 3 | 4 | 10 | 17 | 6 |
| Leicester | 7 | 1 | 2 | 4 | 7 | 12 | 5 |
| Coventry | 7 | 1 | 2 | 4 | 6 | 16 | 5 |
| Everton | 8 | 0 | 3 | 5 | 7 | 18 | 3 |

*Robert Lee celebrates his first goal.*

# *October 5*

BARNSLEY 0

NEWCASTLE 1

*(Half-time score : 0-1)*

*Barnsley:* Watson, Eaden,
Fleming (Liddell 69), Wilson,
Taggart, Davis, O'Connell,
Redfearn, Jackson (Rammell 46),
Payton, Bishop.
*Newcastle:* Srnicek, Hottiger,
Beresford, Howey, Peacock,
Albert, Lee, Clark, Cole, Kitson
(Mathie 85), Sellars.
*Subs:* Watson, Hooper.
*Scorer:* Cole 41.
*Referee:* K Lynch
(Knaresborough).
*Attendance:* 10,992

Andy Cole showed last night that a week of controversy has done nothing to impair his deadly aim.

They say the best strikers require only one chance to show precisely how good they are. Cole's came 41 minutes into this tricky Oakwell assignment and he took it with authority to deliver the Coca-Cola Cup tie into Kevin Keegan's grateful hands.

It was the ideal response from the striker who landed himself in a spot of trouble by complaining about his exclusion from the latest England squad.

It was Cole's 12th goal of the season, not bad for a man who plays on despite being only 80 per cent fit.

The fact that Newcastle did not add to it says much about the level of commitment shown by First Division Barnsley. They restricted Paul Kitson, on his £2.25 million full debut, to one scoring opportunity, which he headed wide.

But, while Cole was the man who put the Premiership leaders into today's third-round draw, England-bound Robert Lee was probably the man of the match. With a bit more luck Lee could have finished with a hat-trick.

Manager Keegan said: "The number of chances we created you would wonder how we came to win only 1-0."

If Cole's strike was not exactly an insult to Barnsley's first-half display, it was still something of an affront, just as on Tyneside a fortnight earlier it was Barnsley who looked the more effective.

Neil Redfearn almost produced a replica of his first-leg goal inside the opening half-hour but was denied by Pavel Srnicek. Until Newcastle scored the Czech keeper was their stabilising force.

And it was an ill-timed stumble from player-boss Danny Wilson which cost Barnsley the chance to catch out the Premiership leaders. Marc Hottiger carved open Barnsley's defence before Lee set up Cole to sweep the ball in.

Lee should have put the tie beyond doubt by half-time. but hit the post after a clever cross from Lee Clark, starting his first senior game of the season.

Afterwards Wilson said: "Newcastle could surpass what Liverpool once did. You don't realise how quick they are until you've played them."

*Arms aloft Cole asks for the praise he deserves.*

# *October 9*

---

## NEWCASTLE 1
## BLACKBURN ROVERS 1
*(Half-time score : 0-0)*

*Newcastle:* Srnicek, Hottiger, Beresford, Howey, Peacock, Watson, Fox, Lee (Kitson 77), Sellars, Beardsley, Cole.
*Subs:* Hooper, Clark.
*Blackburn:* Flowers, Warhurst, Le Saux, Hendry, Berg, Sherwood, Ripley, Atkins, Wilcox, Sutton, Shearer.
*Scorers:* (Newcastle): Flowers 88 og; (Blackburn): Shearer 58 pen.
*Referee:* S Lodge (Barnsley).
*Attendance:* 34,344

There was no Cole delivery at Newcastle yesterday, so young defender Steve Howey unearthed a nugget of his own to keep the flames burning brightly at St James' Park.

Blackburn Rovers were two minutes from inflicting a defeat to douse the fire that has swept through Tyneside this season and bring to an end Kevin Keegan's run of 12 league and cup games without defeat. But, with another full house crowd of 34,206 stoking-up their heroes, United responded with a fixed bayonet charge in the final few minutes to produce an equaliser to Alan Shearer's 58th-minute penalty.

Howey will claim it was his goal, his first for two seasons for the club. The FA, which arbitrates on these matters, may view the video and decide otherwise. For, as the ball fell to the young centre-half in the congestion of the Blackburn penalty area, his shot seemed to be cleared off the line by Jason Wilcox only to strike Tim Flowers and rebound over the line.

At all events it was enough to keep Keegan's unbeaten record intact on an afternoon when the football on the field never quite matched the passion on the terraces.

This might have been due in part to Peter Beardsley being clearly less than fit. And when Robert Lee also failed to make an impact, his mind perhaps drifting to Wednesday's England game against Romania, it left Andy Cole a remote and isolated figure.

None of this should detract from Blackburn's achievement for they had deserved to be the side to end Newcastle's exhilarating run. Their tactic of flying the ball behind the United defence always caused problems.

Blackburn and Newcastle are two traditional old clubs enjoying a renaissance under philanthropic boardrooms, yet it is Keegan, with his extrovert style, who has captured public popularity more than the introvert Kenny Dalglish.

This has given Rovers and their fans a complex about how they are viewed outside their corner of East Lancashire, a belief that it is them against the world, and it has served to heighten their determination.

This was their launch pad for a three-week spell in which they face

Liverpool, Manchester United and Nottingham Forest when their ability to snatch the Premiership from Manchester will be closely scrutinised. It will have given Dalglish some satisfaction that in five attempts Keegan has yet to beat him.

Three of those have been Blackburn victories and a further one seemed likely in this meeting when goalkeeper Pavel Srnicek stuck out a leg to send Wilcox sprawling in the penalty area. Shearer, given a moment to think about it might have felt like Brutus inflicting the fatal sword wound on Julius Caesar as he stood over the penalty kick in front of the Gallowgate End fans with whom he stood shoulder to shoulder a few seasons ago. But the assassin's eye took over and he sent Srnicek the wrong way.

Until then Newcastle had defended stoically, with young Howey handling Shearer with assurance and Steve Watson filling the Barry Venison role in front of the back four with concentrated grit.

Shearer, who idolised Keegan from the terraces here, might have given Blackburn the lead in the third minute but uncharacteristically missed the target with his header from Stuart Ripley's cross.

It was a scrappy first half with space at a premium and players closed down, invention stifled and shots on target intermittent. The decibel count was low from the country's noisiest fans. It soared only in agreement when referee Steve Lodge cautioned first Shearer for taking a shot on goal when the whistle had blown for offside, then Chris Sutton for a tackle when he made no contact with Watson.

Lee might have ended the deadlock when Scott Sellars' corner fell at his feet in the six-yard box but he stumbled. Then Cole received the ball from John Beresford with his back to goal and turned his defender in that lovely muscular way of his to force Flowers into a diving save.

The game needed a goal and Srnicek was cautioned for his part in providing it for Blackburn, relieved no doubt that it was a yellow and not a red card he was shown for his foul on Wilcox.

The score stirred United and they went for Rovers with a vengeance. Lee had a header tipped over by Flowers and Beardsley took the ball on his chest and volleyed against the crossbar.

With Newcastle piling forward it was inevitable they might be caught on the break and Srnicek needed to match Flowers' gymnastics to keep out a Sutton shot and then stand his ground at the near post to Mark Atkins.

Blackburn decided the last 10 minutes were for survival, a fatal mistake for they were defending too deeply and, as the bodies piled into the area, the chances of an equaliser grew. It may have come courtesy of Flowers' backside but Howey was the toast of the locals.

Newcastle now have a two-point advantage over second-placed Nottingham Forest.

Keegan said: "That will be hard for Kenny Dalglish to swallow because Blackburn were a goal up with two minutes to go. I don't think we did enough to win but I don't think we deserved to lose either. "We are both going to be in the shake-up at the end of the season. It's no shame to draw against Blackburn."

Dalglish had no quibble with Lodge's decision to show Srnicek a yellow card and not a red one. "There was no way he deserved to be sent off," said Dalglish. "The incident took place in the far corner of the penalty area."

### League Table After Match

|  | P | W | D | L | F | A | Pts |
|---|---|---|---|---|---|---|---|
| Newcastle | 9 | 7 | 2 | 0 | 26 | 9 | 23 |
| Nottm Forest | 9 | 6 | 3 | 0 | 20 | 10 | 21 |
| Blackburn | 9 | 5 | 3 | 1 | 18 | 6 | 18 |
| Liverpool | 8 | 5 | 2 | 1 | 19 | 7 | 17 |
| Man Utd | 9 | 5 | 1 | 3 | 14 | 7 | 16 |
| Chelsea | 8 | 5 | 0 | 3 | 17 | 10 | 15 |
| Southampton | 9 | 4 | 3 | 2 | 14 | 13 | 15 |
| Norwich | 9 | 4 | 3 | 2 | 7 | 7 | 15 |
| Leeds | 9 | 4 | 2 | 3 | 12 | 10 | 14 |
| Tottenham | 9 | 4 | 1 | 4 | 15 | 17 | 13 |
| Man City | 9 | 3 | 3 | 3 | 14 | 13 | 12 |
| Arsenal | 9 | 3 | 2 | 4 | 11 | 10 | 11 |
| West Ham | 9 | 3 | 2 | 4 | 5 | 10 | 11 |
| Aston Villa | 9 | 2 | 3 | 4 | 10 | 13 | 9 |
| Wimbledon | 9 | 2 | 3 | 4 | 7 | 12 | 9 |
| Sheff Wed | 9 | 2 | 3 | 4 | 11 | 17 | 9 |
| QPR | 9 | 1 | 4 | 4 | 12 | 16 | 7 |
| Ipswich | 8 | 2 | 1 | 5 | 9 | 15 | 7 |
| C Palace | 9 | 1 | 4 | 4 | 6 | 13 | 7 |
| Leicester | 9 | 1 | 3 | 5 | 9 | 18 | 6 |
| Coventry | 8 | 1 | 3 | 4 | 8 | 18 | 6 |
| Everton | 9 | 0 | 3 | 6 | 7 | 20 | 3 |

# *October 15*

Kevin Keegan was in full flow in his appreciation of Peter Beardsley when he suggested the little man could shine anywhere, from St James' Park to Moscow.

Why Moscow? Because it was there that Beardsley was relegated to a B team appearance and signed off as an international player by Graham Taylor, then England manager. Taylor later called it all a mis-understanding. Keegan clearly viewed it as a major mistake, and one could see his point after Beardsley's brief moment of goal-scoring poetry had opened a five-point gap at the top of the Premiership.

Choosing his comment carefully when asked if England missed Beardsley through injury against Romania last week, Keegan said: "I didn't see anyone that night with as much to offer."

After Beardsley's last-minute strike in this game – he shimmied in front of a packed defence before threading home a superb drive – Keegan jumped to his feet. Then, seeing Palace's injured player-coach Ray Wilkins on the opposing bench, he gestured towards Beardsley and called over: "That's what England thought they could do without for years." It prompted no argument from the evergreen Wilkins.

"When you've played at that level like Ray, you know what I'm talk-ing about," said Keegan. "Peter makes other players play. Terry Venables knows what he can give a team. He is on a wavelength few players reach. He is a little box of tricks and he is a brave lad. He is not scared to tackle. "How long can Peter Beardsley go on? As long as Peter Beardsley wants to. As long as he is fit. He loves the game. It's the best signing I've ever made. If anyone was made for a team and a team for him, that man was Peter Beardsley and that team was Newcastle."

Palace, who contributed much and deserved better, cursed the mar-riage and Keegan admitted: "I had the gut feeling it would take a sen-sational goal to settle it."

But, after five straight wins away from home, he reacted firmly to suggestions of luck. "We've played the best football in the Premiership this season," he said. "We're a good side, not a lucky one. When I played for Liverpool we won a lot of games in the last five minutes."

Striker Paul Kitson, starting his first league game since his £2.25 mil-

---

**CRYSTAL PALACE 0**

**NEWCASTLE 1**

*(Half-time score : 0-0)*

*Palace:* Martyn, Humphrey, Gordon, Southgate, Coleman, Armstrong, Salako, Shaw, Bowry, Preece, Newman.
*Newcastle:* Srnicek, Beresford, Fox, Howey, Beardsley, Cole, Sellars, Watson, Neilson, Albert, Kitson.
*Subs:* Clark, Drysdale, Hooper.
*Scorer:* Beardsley 89.
*Referee:* K Morton (Bury St Edmunds).
*Attendance:* 17,760

## League Table After Match

| | P | W | D | L | F | A | Pts |
|---|---|---|---|---|---|---|---|
| Newcastle | 10 | 8 | 2 | 0 | 27 | 9 | 26 |
| Blackburn | 10 | 6 | 3 | 1 | 21 | 8 | 21 |
| Nottm Forest | 9 | 6 | 3 | 0 | 20 | 10 | 21 |
| Man Utd | 10 | 6 | 1 | 3 | 15 | 7 | 19 |
| Liverpool | 9 | 5 | 2 | 2 | 21 | 10 | 17 |
| Norwich | 10 | 4 | 4 | 2 | 8 | 8 | 16 |
| Chelsea | 9 | 5 | 0 | 4 | 18 | 13 | 15 |
| Man City | 10 | 4 | 3 | 3 | 16 | 14 | 15 |
| Leeds | 10 | 4 | 3 | 3 | 13 | 11 | 15 |
| Southampton | 10 | 4 | 3 | 3 | 17 | 17 | 15 |
| Arsenal | 10 | 4 | 2 | 4 | 14 | 11 | 14 |
| Tottenham | 10 | 4 | 2 | 4 | 16 | 18 | 14 |
| Sheff Wed | 10 | 3 | 3 | 4 | 13 | 18 | 12 |
| Coventry | 10 | 3 | 3 | 4 | 12 | 18 | 12 |
| West Ham | 10 | 3 | 2 | 5 | 5 | 11 | 11 |
| Aston Villa | 10 | 2 | 4 | 4 | 11 | 14 | 10 |
| Wimbledon | 9 | 2 | 3 | 4 | 7 | 12 | 9 |
| Leicester | 10 | 2 | 3 | 5 | 12 | 21 | 9 |
| QPR | 10 | 1 | 4 | 5 | 13 | 18 | 7 |
| C Palace | 10 | 1 | 4 | 5 | 6 | 14 | 7 |
| Ipswich | 10 | 2 | 1 | 7 | 10 | 19 | 7 |
| Everton | 10 | 0 | 3 | 7 | 7 | 22 | 3 |

lion transfer from Derby, said: "If you can't play in this team you can't play."

Time will tell whether the wind and mud of approaching winter will bog down Keegan's Toon Army. But the Newcastle manager revealed that chairman Sir John Hall would not cut the supply line. "If I need another player I know I've only to pick up the phone and I'll get one thousand per cent support," he said.

Palace manager Alan Smith, on more limited resources, could take comfort from the performance of his youngsters and Keegan's prediction that they were too good to go down.

Had skipper Gareth Southgate been blessed with good fortune, he would have given Palace the lead. Much later, had Chris Armstrong given depth and not height to a header from a John Salako cross, Newcastle goalkeeper Pavel Srnicek would have been beaten. But Ruel Fox and Kitson had similar complaints at the other end.

*"If anyone was made for a team and a team for him, that man was Peter Beardsley and that team was Newcastle".*

# *October 18*

Newcastle put down their deposit on a place in the last 16 of the Uefa Cup but a nightmare final 20 minutes left them looking far from certain to collect.

It all went so well at first for Kevin Keegan's Premiership leaders as they showed how well they are adjusting to the new world of Europe. Ruel Fox scored after nine minutes of this second-round first leg to settle Newcastle on a night when they feared frustration would be their biggest enemy.

Skipper Peter Beardsley cracked Newcastle's second from the penalty spot 11 minutes before half-time and Andy Cole headed a third 11 minutes into the second half.

But Bilbao striker Jose Ziganda, whose pace troubled Newcastle all night, scored a crucial away goal for the Spaniards with 19 minutes left. And the substitute Gonzalo Suances stunned St James' Park with a second Spanish goal 11 minutes from time.

Keegan said: "We were all over them for 60 minutes but we committed a little bit of suicide. It was all over at 3-0 but a combination of things changed all that. They started to chance their arm and we became a bit naive.

"What we needed was a Barry Venison or Paul Bracewell out there in the last 20 minutes, somebody who would have said, 'We're going to hang on to this'. I have told them a few home truths but I have also looked at myself. Maybe I should have thrown a defender on but it's easy to be wise after the event."

Fox gave Newcastle that priceless early lead after John Beresford headed a long ball from Scott Sellars across the area. The ball was nudged on by Cole and, although Fox hardly caught it sweetly, his shot squirted through the hands of Bilbao goalkeeper Juan Valencia.

The Spaniards, though, had genuine pace up front. Ziganda got in front of central defender Steve Howey, whose nudge on the striker raised penalty possibilities that German referee Helmut Krug dismissed.

Newcastle's patient search for a second goal was rewarded with a penalty, awarded when Cole went down under a challenge from defender Oscea Tebuenka.

NEWCASTLE **3**

ATHLETIC BILBAO **2**

*(Half-time score : 2-0)*

*Newcastle:* Srnicek, Hottiger, Beresford, Peacock, Howey, Albert, Fox, Beardsley, Cole, Clark, Sellars.
*Bilbao:* Valencia, Tebuenka (Suances 67), Larrazabal, Karanka, Andrinua, Vales, Estibariz (Korino 84), Alkiza, Ziganda, Garitano, Mendiguren.
*Scorers:* (Newcastle): Fox 9 Beardsley 34 pen, Cole 56; (Athletic): Ziganda 71, Suances 79,
*Referee:* H Krug (Germany).
*Attendance:* 32,140

In 19 months at Newcastle Cole has not gone more than two games without scoring and he kept up that record. His goal was the climax of a slick move, Newcastle's best of the match. Beardsley and Lee Clark exchanged passes and, when Fox crossed, Cole placed his header perfectly beyond Valencia's reach. It was his 66th goal in 71 starts for Newcastle.

The away goals Keegan did not want to concede arrived when Suances put Ziganda through to shoot home and then headed in himself from Ricardo Mendiguren's cross.

*Andy Cole butts in Newcastle's third against Athletic Bilbao.*

# *October 22*

Scott Sellars, playing well enough to earn recommendations for an England call-up, confessed what no budding international should confess. Having enjoyed another outstanding Saturday, United's little man at the top said: "I thought I wasn't going to be good enough for the Premiership."

That fear festered in him before he left Leeds 19 months ago. "I hardly got a game in my second spell at Leeds and that left my confidence absolutely shot," said Sellars. "But Kevin Keegan has given me self-belief."

One could see that in the way he played in midfield, as Wednesday became the latest side to fail to dent Newcastle's unbeaten record, despite strong late pressure. Sellars' prized left foot set up Andy Cole's 14th goal of the season, adding to the earlier one that Philippe Albert and Steve Watson are still arguing about as to actual ownership.

Keegan, who had already supplied Terry Venables with new internationals in Barry Venison and Robert Lee this season, does not doubt for one moment that Sellars is good enough. "We know he's not going to win headers against John Fashanu but he can open up any defence.

"If he was called upon by England that wouldn't bother him. In fact he would probably be even more comfortable at that level."

Wednesday aren't comfortable at all, not while they wait for confirmation on the extent of David Hirst's knee damage. Though substitute Chris Bart-Williams performed as well as anyone in his role as an emergency striker, manager Trevor Francis desperately needs a fit Hirst for the Coca-Cola Cup tie against Southampton on Wednesday.

"I am hoping it's good news because it would be a big blow to lose him for any length of time," he said.

Yet he has every reason to be encouraged by the way his team came back at Newcastle having been two down at half-time. And, while Ian Taylor's first Premiership goal owed much to an embarrassing slip from goalkeeper Pavel Srnicek, they still created plenty of match-saving opportunities.

Andy Sinton, who as a schoolboy turned down the chance to join Newcastle, thought Wednesday might just have done enough to

---

**NEWCASTLE 2**

**SHEFF WED 1**

*(Half-time score : 2-0)*

*Newcastle:* Srnicek, Hottiger, Beresford, Watson, Albert, Peacock, Fox, Bearsdley, Cole, Clark, Sellars.
*Subs:* Mathie, Hooper.
*Sheff Wed:* Pressman, Atherton (Petrescu 65), Nolan, Taylor, Pearce, Walker, Hyde, Bright, Hirst (Bart-Williams 29), Sheridan, Sinton.
*Scorers:* (Newcastle): Watson 35, Cole 37; (Sheff Wed): Taylor 55.
*Referee:* G Poll (Tilehurst).
*Attendance:* 34,408

| | P | W | D | L | F | A | Pts |
|---|---|---|---|---|---|---|---|
| Newcastle........... | 11 | 9 | 2 | 0 | 29 | 10 | 29 |
| Nottm Forest.... | 11 | 8 | 3 | 0 | 25 | 11 | 27 |
| Man Utd............ | 11 | 7 | 1 | 3 | 19 | 9 | 22 |
| Blackburn........... | 11 | 6 | 3 | 2 | 23 | 12 | 21 |
| Liverpool......... | 10 | 6 | 2 | 2 | 24 | 10 | 20 |
| Norwich............. | 11 | 5 | 4 | 2 | 12 | 10 | 19 |
| Chelsea.............. | 10 | 6 | 0 | 4 | 20 | 13 | 18 |
| Man City............ | 11 | 5 | 3 | 3 | 21 | 16 | 18 |
| Arsenal............. | 11 | 5 | 2 | 4 | 16 | 12 | 17 |
| Leeds................. | 10 | 4 | 3 | 3 | 13 | 11 | 15 |
| Southampton..... | 11 | 4 | 3 | 4 | 17 | 19 | 15 |
| West Ham........... | 11 | 4 | 2 | 5 | 7 | 11 | 14 |
| Tottenham.......... | 11 | 4 | 2 | 5 | 18 | 23 | 14 |
| Sheff Wed.......... | 11 | 3 | 2 | 5 | 14 | 20 | 12 |
| Coventry............. | 11 | 3 | 3 | 5 | 13 | 20 | 12 |
| Aston Villa........ | 11 | 2 | 4 | 5 | 11 | 16 | 10 |
| C Palace............ | 11 | 2 | 4 | 5 | 7 | 14 | 10 |
| Leicester............. | 10 | 2 | 3 | 5 | 13 | 21 | 9 |
| Wimbledon......... | 11 | 2 | 3 | 6 | 8 | 18 | 9 |
| QPR.................... | 11 | 1 | 4 | 6 | 15 | 22 | 7 |
| Ipswich............. | 11 | 2 | 1 | 8 | 10 | 21 | 7 |
| Everton.............. | 11 | 0 | 2 | 8 | 7 | 23 | 3 |

extend their short unbeaten run and give the leaders a jolt before the first of two big meetings with Manchester United.

But Sinton had to admit: "They are a very good side and there's no reason why they can't go all the way. If we aren't going to win the League, nothing would give me greater pleasure than to see Newcastle do it."

*Andy Cole gets in a header despite the attentions of Des Walker.*

# *October 26*

Philippe Albert, the straight-backed Belgian with the guardsman's gait, applied the bayonet to the reserve side that Manchester United sent to Newcastle.

A flock of Fergie Fledglings, including five teenagers, had spread their wings at St James' Park and Kevin Keegan's side had looked increasingly frustrated. There were only eight minutes left when Swiss international Marc Hottiger crossed from the right and Albert soared to head his first goal for the club.

With the breakthrough achieved and United committed to seek an equaliser, Paul Kitson helped himself to his first goal since moving to the club from Derby County.

This was a result that really suits all parties. Ferguson has made no secret of the fact he viewed the Coca-Cola Cup as an inhibition to his European Cup and Premier League ambitions. He made the right noises after the game when he said: "We don't like to lose any game but I am masking it quite well. If we are going to do well in other tournaments this season we have to spread our staff a little bit.

"It was difficult for Newcastle because they expected me to play the older players. But I hope they do well in the competition because they have been a breath of fresh air this season. They have played their football the right way."

It was a night for mutual respect. Keegan was ready to praise the quality of the youngsters Fergie has unearthed. "When you looked at the line-ups it seemed they were fielding a side we might overrun," he said. "But they have some very good youngsters and we had to fight all the way."

For United there was still a price to pay from this absorbing and competitive game. Lee Sharpe, who came on as second-half substitute, is out of Saturday's Premier League meeting between the sides at Old Trafford. Denis Irwin, the man he replaced, has a knee injury and Nicky Butt also finished the game limping with knee trouble, a worrying situation with Barcelona to face in the Champions League next week. Ferguson's concern must have been offset by the mature performances he received in midfield from Butt and the impressive David Beckham while Keith Gillespie looks as if he could stand in if Sharpe

**NEWCASTLE 2**

**MANCHESTER UNITED 0**

*(Half-time score : 0-0)*

*Newcastle:* Srnicek, Hottiger, Beresford, Howey, Peacock, Albert, Beardsley, Watson, Sellars, Cole (Guppy 63), Kitson.
*Subs:* Hooper, Clark.
*United:* Walsh, Neville, Irwin (Sharpe 51), Bruce, Butt, Pallister, Gillespie, Beckham, McClair, Scholes, Davies.
*Scorers:* Albert 82, Kitson 87
*Referee:* T Holbrook (Walsall).
*Attendance:* 34,178

and Ryan Giggs are ruled out.

Newcastle will not lose many games in their splendid citadel, once again bulging with a crowd of 34,178 inside, and this victory, their 17th consecutive match unbeaten since the start of the season, sets a record. They play their football with a refreshing, open style and, but for the courageous defending of Steve Bruce in the opening 15 minutes, this contest might not have been in suspense for so long. With Peter Beardsley endlessly probing, Scott Sellars looking like a marathon runner and Kitson anxious to prove his muscular pedigree there was bound to come a time when Ferguson's kids would tire.

It turned out to be a great night for Albert and his jubilation at scoring his first goal fitted the festival atmosphere. "I'm pleased for him because he has had to play in just about every position except the one I bought him for," said Keegan. "And I was pleased to see Kitson get his first goal because he is a very exciting lad."

*Paul Kitson threads a way through United's defence.*

# October 29

This was not so much a game of football as an eloquent statement of intent. The message, simply, is that it is dangerous to mess with Manchester United.

The question posed – no sleaze money required – was whether Newcastle were serious contenders for the seat of power in the Premiership. Kevin Keegan's side were chastened by the response.

They had crossed the Pennines hoping to return with a 10-point advantage on the champions. Instead they must look over their shoulders at the pursuing pack, a mere six points separating first from fifth, at a time when their early supremacy comes under scrutiny.

Managers tend to assess games on a scale of one to three, depending on the number of points collected. Just occasionally they can leave empty-handed but full of heart.

Keegan is an optimist – and ambassador, too. His disappointment at seeing a marvellous unbeaten 18-match run ended was offset by the knowledge that his side had richly contributed to a contest of epic entertainment.

"It was a terrific game," he said. "The pace of it took your breath away. Great atmosphere. Great surface. Great players. Wrong result. The consolation for me is that we have come here and played them the way we wanted to play them. We have showed some character. But they are good, everybody knows that.

"Whoever wins the League has to beat them. I have been saying that every week, so I am not going to say any different having lost here. In the last 25 minutes, when they were 2-0 up, they were exceptional."

Without the injured Andy Cole and Paul Kitson, and against a defence as parsimonious as Alex Ferguson's, it would have been easy for Keegan to stock up in midfield. That would have been a betrayal of his principles, though, and it is one of Keegan's more endearing qualities that he is in the forefront of the crusade to make soccer more appealing.

He knew the champions are most comfortable against teams that come at them because they can then maximise the pace they have in forward positions. Keegan said: "They really do break at pace. They like teams to come on to them and we didn't let them down."

## MANCHESTER UNITED 2
### NEWCASTLE 0
*(Half-time score : 1-0)*

*United:* Schmeichel, Keane, Irwin, Bruce, Kanchelskis, Pallister, Cantona, Ince, McClair, Hughes, Giggs (Gillespie 66).
*Newcastle:* Srnicek, Hottiger (Mathie 75), Beresford, Albert, Peacock, Howey, Watson, Beardsley, Lee, Fox (Clark 75), Sellars.
*Sub:* Hooper.
*Scorers:* Pallister 11, Gillespie 77.
*Referee:* J B Worrall (Warrington).
*Attendance:* 43,795

Newcastle took the gamble and paid the price. But in the meantime they enhanced their reputation as a side of genuine adventure. It should surprise nobody that the gates are locked each time they play. That has been the case with Manchester United for some years now.

As they brace themselves for Barcelona this week, Ferguson has the assurance that his defence has been extended as it might expect to be in the Nou Camp.

"I knew Newcastle would try to beat us," he said. "So often teams come here just to frustrate us. When that happens you tend not to have to sweat too much defensively. Newcastle make you sweat. Some of their last-third play is excellent, one-touch football around the edge of the area and you really have to be alert to it."

There was some superb interplay between Robert Lee and Peter Beardsley but the test would have been stiffer with Cole on the end of it and Keegan admitted: "We were a toothless tiger and never really had the penetration we normally have. I think if Alex lost Mark Hughes he would have a problem up front. There are not many of those type around: Cole, Hughes, Ferdinand, Wright, Shearer, Sutton. That's why people pay £5m for them."

With Paul Ince moving through the gears like Damon Hill and Andrei Kanchelskis showing the pace that would make him a favourite in the Greyhound Derby, United were a spectacle to behold.

"Some of our attacking play was magnificent," said Ferguson. "I think Pavel Srnicek has probably had his best-ever game. The pace of our play was a great advert for the game. We tend to overlook that factor. When you see tremendous skills exhibited at that speed, then you get the excitement."

Young Ulsterman Keith Gillespie, a replacement after an hour for a muted Ryan Giggs, scored a goal which served only to underline the richness of the seam at Old Trafford. That, perhaps, is the difference between the champions and the pretenders – no Cole, no goal. United, on the other hand, are spreading the scoring load.

Yet Fergie has his own headache now, that of selecting the side to face Barcelona. He says he will bring Paul Parker in at right-back and move Roy Keane, who played well there in this game, into midfield.

If he plays Peter Schmeichel, Denis Irwin and Keane, however, Giggs will have to sit it out. It is the old game of musical chairs. He must hope the music he plays it to has the same high notes it reached on Saturday.

### League Table After Match

|              | P  | W | D | L | F  | A  | Pts |
|--------------|----|---|---|---|----|----|-----|
| Newcastle    | 12 | 9 | 2 | 1 | 29 | 12 | 29  |
| Nottm Forest | 12 | 8 | 3 | 1 | 25 | 13 | 27  |
| Man Utd      | 12 | 8 | 1 | 3 | 21 | 9  | 25  |
| Blackburn    | 12 | 7 | 3 | 2 | 25 | 12 | 24  |
| Liverpool    | 11 | 7 | 2 | 2 | 27 | 11 | 23  |
| Leeds        | 12 | 6 | 3 | 3 | 18 | 13 | 21  |
| Chelsea      | 11 | 6 | 1 | 4 | 21 | 14 | 19  |
| Norwich      | 12 | 5 | 4 | 3 | 12 | 11 | 19  |
| Man City     | 12 | 5 | 3 | 4 | 21 | 17 | 18  |
| Arsenal      | 12 | 5 | 3 | 4 | 17 | 13 | 18  |
| Tottenham    | 12 | 5 | 2 | 5 | 21 | 24 | 17  |
| Southampton  | 12 | 4 | 3 | 5 | 18 | 22 | 15  |
| Coventry     | 12 | 4 | 3 | 5 | 14 | 20 | 15  |
| West Ham     | 12 | 4 | 2 | 6 | 8  | 14 | 14  |
| Sheff Wed    | 12 | 3 | 4 | 5 | 15 | 21 | 13  |
| C Palace     | 12 | 3 | 4 | 5 | 8  | 14 | 13  |
| Wimbledon    | 12 | 3 | 3 | 6 | 9  | 18 | 12  |
| QPR          | 12 | 2 | 4 | 6 | 17 | 22 | 10  |
| Aston Villa  | 12 | 2 | 4 | 6 | 11 | 18 | 10  |
| Leicester    | 12 | 2 | 3 | 7 | 14 | 24 | 9   |
| Ipswich      | 12 | 2 | 1 | 9 | 11 | 24 | 7   |
| Everton      | 12 | 0 | 4 | 8 | 8  | 24 | 4   |

*Robert Lee avoids Ince's sliding tackle.*

# *November 1*

---

**ATHLETIC BILBAO 1**

**NEWCASTLE 0**

*(Half-time score : 0-0
Agg. score: 3-3, Bilbao
win on away goals)*

---

*Bilbao:* Valencia, Tebuenka, Larrazabal, Karanka, Andrinua, Larrainzar (Urrutia 31), Suances, Alkiza, Ziganda, Garitano, Mendiguren.
*Newcastle:* Srnicek, Hottiger, Beresford, Albert, Peacock, Howey, Lee, Beardsley, Watson, Fox (Jeffrey 72), Sellars (Clark 58).
*Subs:* Parker, Pilkington.
*Scorer:* Ziganda 67.
*Referee:* A Amendolia (Italy).
*Attendance:* 47,000

---

Kevin Keegan crashed out of Europe with Newcastle United last night but promised: "We will be back." The Premiership leaders failed to make it through to Friday's Uefa Cup third-round draw after going out on the away goals rule.

But the United manager made it clear that he is looking to make a speedy return. Keegan said: "It is my job to make sure that we qualify for these games again next year. It is going to be difficult but that is our aim."

Keegan would not blame Pavel Srnicek for failing to keep out Jose Ziganda's vital 67th-minute strike, which slipped under the keeper's body. Although Keegan said it should have been stopped, he pointed out that a deflection off Steve Howey played a part in the goal.

Despite believing that Newcastle should have been awarded a late penalty for a foul on Robert Lee, Keegan refused to criticise Italian referee Angelo Amendolia. He agreed that Newcastle threw it all away on Tyneside two weeks ago when they allowed Bilbao to dismantle their three-goal lead with two late strikes.

Keegan mused: "We should have been coming here to eat some paella, then enjoy the game. But I give credit to Bilbao. They found the spirit to come back in the first game. I hope they go on and win the competition. I said it would be an adventure. We did not know when it would end. We do now."

Newcastle had attempted to achieve the impossible and keep 45,000 Basques quiet. For more than half this tie that is exactly what they did. Srnicek had only two genuine saves to make in the opening 45 minutes.

Bilbao played much good, one-touch football, but, impressive as it looked, there was not a lot at the end of those moves thanks to excellent Newcastle covering.

Keegan had decided this was not the moment for budding young striker Paul Brayson. Instead he pushed utility man Steve Watson up alongside skipper Peter Beardsley and asked him to forage for all he was worth.

Newcastle's best chance of the first half fell to Robert Lee when Beardsley picked him out with a stunning, diagonal pass. But Lee could not find instant control and was crowded out by goalkeeper Juan Valencia.

Lee thought he had won a penalty when he was brought down just inside the Bilbao penalty area, but the referee waved away appeals. In the last minute Beardsley almost produced a lifesaver, forcing a magnificent save from Valencia.

In that final frenetic 20 minutes Newcastle also enjoyed good fortune. The Spaniards had the chance to go through in more convincing fashion when John Beresford handed Bilbao a penalty by bringing down first-leg hero Gonzalo Suances. But Ander Garitano's shot hit a post and, although he put the rebound away, it was disallowed for an illegal second touch.

*The despair of defeat sinks in as Howey sits bewildered on the deserted pitch.*

# *November 5*

---

### NEWCASTLE 2
### QPR 1
*(Half-time score : 2-0)*

*Newcastle:* Srnicek, Hottiger, Beresford, Albert, Howey, Peacock, Fox, Lee, Kitson, Beardsley, Watson.
*Subs:* Clark, Neilson, Hooper
*QPR:* Dykstra, Bardsley, Wilson, Barker, McDonald, Yates, Impey, Hodge (Dichio 50), Ferdinand, Gallen, Sinclair.
*Scorers:* (Newcastle): Kitson 20, Beardsley 42; (QPR): Dichio 60.
*Referee:* G Ashby (Worcester).
*Attendance:* 34,278

Kevin Keegan believes QPR should make sure they keep Gerry Francis. Otherwise put your money on Les Ferdinand following him out of the Loftus Road door.

Ferdinand dodged the big issue – his own future – with the stealth he would like to have found to knock the Premiership leaders off their perch. But between the lines of what Ferdy is and is not saying the message is clear enough.

"We are all part of a team here and everyone would be disappointed if Gerry left," said the £5 million-rated striker. Year in, year out, we've had members of the team taken away and if he left we would lose another important team member. When I signed a new contract in the summer it was in the belief that Gerry would be staying. We had a chat and both knew what we wanted from the season."

So, if Francis goes, will Ferdy want to do the same? "I can't really answer that," he said. Why not? "I don't want to. I don't want to add to the turmoil."

To Keegan it was all vaguely familiar. His Newcastle team now go to Forest hoping to increase a two-point championship lead but more often than not they have been where Rangers are now: at odds with themselves.

The Newcastle manager said: "In a way these are the problems this club had for what seemed like an eternity. If common sense prevails, Gerry Francis will still be with them next week because he's got so much to offer. But, as we know, common sense doesn't always prevail."

Quality tends to though, which is why Peter Beardsley made sure Newcastle kept second-placed Blackburn at arm's length. The United captain forged an interesting partnership with Paul Kitson, who scored a stylish first league goal since moving from Derby for £2.25m. Good as it was, Beardsley bettered it shortly before half-time with an acrobatic overhead volley.

It was a timely reminder to Terry Venables as the England coach settled down to assembling a squad for the Nigerians. Keegan is sure Beardsley will be in that squad and sees him as a key man in the build-up to the European Championship.

"It would be great news for Newcastle," he said. "It will keep Peter bubbling along. He's got that target to aim at internationally. I had it taken away from me towards the end of my career and, no matter how much you enjoy football, it's never quite the same."

Yet what will encourage Forest at the City Ground is the certain knowledge that, no matter how many problems the leaders cause you at one end, they always give opponents a chance at the other.

Francis, who obviously fancied a going-away present from Rangers, even though they were two-down at half-time, almost got one following his swift team reshuffle.

The introduction of 20-year-old Daniele Dichio five minutes into the second half did the trick as Rangers took over a game Newcastle had dominated. Dichio scored for the second Saturday running and his team-mates ought to have added to it. Steve Howey's excellent covering work and the goalkeeping of under-rated Pavel Srnicek made sure they did not.

It left Francis saying: "I don't know whether this was my last match. If so, then I am intensely proud of my players. We showed against Liverpool and again today that we can compete with the best and it's hard to come away with nothing."

### League Table After Match

| | P | W | D | L | F | A | Pts |
|---|---|---|---|---|---|---|---|
| Newcastle | 13 | 10 | 2 | 1 | 31 | 13 | 32 |
| Blackburn | 14 | 9 | 3 | 2 | 28 | 12 | 30 |
| Man Utd | 13 | 9 | 1 | 3 | 23 | 10 | 28 |
| Nottm Forest | 13 | 8 | 3 | 2 | 25 | 14 | 27 |
| Liverpool | 13 | 8 | 2 | 3 | 29 | 13 | 26 |
| Leeds | 14 | 7 | 3 | 4 | 21 | 16 | 24 |
| Norwich | 14 | 5 | 6 | 3 | 13 | 12 | 21 |
| Chelsea | 12 | 6 | 2 | 4 | 23 | 16 | 20 |
| Man City | 13 | 5 | 4 | 4 | 24 | 20 | 19 |
| Arsenal | 13 | 5 | 4 | 4 | 17 | 13 | 19 |
| C Palace | 14 | 5 | 4 | 5 | 15 | 15 | 19 |
| Southampton | 14 | 4 | 5 | 5 | 22 | 26 | 17 |
| Tottenham | 13 | 5 | 2 | 6 | 21 | 26 | 17 |
| West Ham | 14 | 5 | 2 | 7 | 9 | 15 | 17 |
| Coventry | 14 | 4 | 4 | 6 | 17 | 26 | 16 |
| Sheff Wed | 14 | 3 | 5 | 6 | 15 | 22 | 14 |
| QPR | 14 | 3 | 4 | 7 | 20 | 25 | 13 |
| Wimbledon | 13 | 3 | 3 | 7 | 10 | 21 | 12 |
| Aston Villa | 13 | 2 | 4 | 7 | 12 | 20 | 10 |
| Ipswich | 14 | 3 | 1 | 10 | 13 | 27 | 10 |
| Leicester | 13 | 2 | 3 | 8 | 14 | 25 | 9 |
| Everton | 14 | 1 | 5 | 8 | 9 | 24 | 8 |

*Paul Kitson passing Hodge and an airborne Beardsley.*

# *November 7*

---

**NOTTINGHAM FOREST 0**

**NEWCASTLE 0**

*(Half-time score : 0-0)*

*Forest:* Crossley, Lyttle, Pearce, Cooper, Chettle, Phillips, Stone, Bohinen, Woan (Black 77), Collymore, Roy.
*Newcastle:* Srnicek, Beresford, Fox, Lee, Beardsley, Hottiger, Clark, Peacock, Watson, Albert, Kitson.
*Subs:* Mathie, Neilson, Hooper.
*Referee:* K Burge (Tonypandy).
*Attendance:* 22,102

Kevin Keegan took a deep breath last night and insisted: "We can handle the pressure." Newcastle came out of their 21st game of the season unscathed and three points clear at the top of the Premiership.

Keegan said: "On average we've been playing a game every three days but we've handled it. Now we've got a bit of a break. I'm a hard man, so the lads will be in for a bit of training, but there will be a lot of golf involved as well."

Paul Kitson had three chances to stretch Newcastle's lead by a further two points by beating Forest but wasted them and Keegan admitted: "Although we had lots of possession it wasn't until the second half that we made Forest's goalkeeper work for his money."

The bad news for Keegan is that top scorer Andy Cole expects to be out of action for at least another six weeks. He sees a specialist for a check on his shin-splints injury on Friday but expects to be told to continue with the rest cure that has been prescribed.

Forest boss Frank Clark was not too upset after his side failed to wreck Newcastle's title charge. Clark, 11 years on Tyneside as a player, admits he would like to see Keegan's men win the Premiership if Forest fail. "If it's not us, then I want it to be Newcastle," he said.

Clark gambled on playing England hopeful Stan Collymore in an attempt to beat the league leaders. Marksman Collymore convinced Clark yesterday he was fit enough to return to action after a hamstring injury but he failed to tip the balance in Forest's favour.

Darren Peacock had to stop him with a desperate tackle in the sixth minute at the expense of a corner after Lars Bohinen and Bryan Roy closed in. On the half-hour Collymore sent a long pass to Roy, who beat his marker but smashed his shot inches over.

Yet Newcastle were unlucky not to take the lead in the 18th minute when Belgian Philippe Albert met Ruel Fox's corner and Kitson hit a difficult half-volley that Forest full-back Des Lyttle cleared.

Both teams needed to win. Newcastle were out to prove they could recover after losing to Manchester United in the league, going out of Europe and losing top marksman Cole through injury. For Forest there was the incentive to show they have the quality of a championship team.

In the second half Newcastle's Peter Beardsley tested Mark Crossley after good work by Kitson who also saw an effort go just wide.

*Stan Collymore holds off Darren Peacock.*

# November 19

---

### WIMBLEDON 3
### NEWCASTLE 2
*(Half-time score : 3-2)*

*Wimbledon:* Segers, Barton (Fitzgerald 89), Cunningham, Jones, Reeves, Clarke, Ekoku, Goodman (Harford 16), Thorn, Leonhardsen, Elkins.
*Newcastle:* Srnicek, Venison, Beresford, Fox, Howey, Lee, Beardsley, Hottiger, Peacock (Clark 90), Albert, Kitson (Watson 59).
*Sub:* Hooper.
*Scorers:* (Wimbledon): Clarke 2, Ekoku 27, Harford 36; (Newcastle): Beardsley 30, Kitson 32.
*Referee:* P Don (Hanworth Park).
*Attendance:* 14,203

Sam Hammam handed over the readies to Sir John Hall before the kick-off at Selhurst Park – two bags containing £1,000 in £1 coins.

The exchange between Wimbledon's colourful owner and Newcastle's multi-millionaire chairman was captured on camera but there was no hint of boardroom sleaze. Hammam was simply settling a wager laid at the last Footballer of the Year dinner when, on the strength of Wimbledon's sixth-place finish, he claimed his Dons would finish above Sir John's Geordies this season.

He explained: "I bumped into Sir John at the Footballer of the Year dinner at the end of last season. We had finished sixth and Newcastle third. I told him I thought Wimbledon would finish higher than Newcastle this season.

"He asked if I wanted to bet on it and I said I'd gamble £500," said Hammam. "Later that evening he asked if I was prepared to increase the stakes to £1,000. It was a matter of pride. I had to accept and after Newcastle's start to the season I was prepared to concede defeat.

"I asked the bank for £1,000 out of my personal account in – £1 coins for a joke. I had a photograph taken of me handing over the money. But now I'm wondering whether I was little premature."

Hammam's doubts were understandable after Wimbledon's pulsating victory, which consigned Newcastle to a second Premiership defeat and kept them winless in away clashes against Wimbledon.

Hammam's anger at the performance of World Cup referee Phil Don – shared by manager Joe Kinnear and the red-carded Vinnie Jones – gained a sympathetic hearing after nine yellow cards were shown in this match. A summit between soccer's top brass had last week urged officials to show more consistency. But Mr Don's display hardly eased concern.

Jones, not one usually to generate sympathy, deserved it on this occasion after being harshly booked for the second time in the 73rd minute.

Barry Venison, back after two months of hamstring trouble, had motivated Wimbledon – as if they ever needed it – with a pre-match swipe at Jones. Still smarting from last season's 4-2 defeat at Selhurst Park, Venison talked of a "passionate feeling" about this clash.

Venison acted out that passion in three incidents which miraculously went unpunished. They started with a challenge which ended Jon Goodman's debut after 16 minutes and left the Dons' striker needing 16 stitches down his leg.

A lunge at Efan Ekoku followed, retaliatory action from Gary Elkins and the Nigerian striker's dissent prompting the first two bookings of the afternoon. And even when he hacked down Warren Barton for a penalty three minutes before the end of scheduled time Venison still avoided a card of any colour.

Jones said: "We had eight bookings, yet Venison didn't get anything. Perhaps someone can explain to me what's going on. People will say Vinnie has been sent off but it would be better if they said Vinnie was captain and we beat Newcastle again."

Despite the referee's intervention, this was a game of rich endeavour, amazing goalmouth action and astute football. "Our aim is to finish better than the sixth place we had last season," said Kinnear, who has compiled an outfit capable of achieving that aim.

Andy Clarke hit the first after only a minute and his cross was deflected against the post before Ekoku slotted in the second after 27 minutes.

Newcastle's response was emphatic and in five minutes they were level. Peter Beardsley pulled one back and was instrumental in providing Paul Kitson with the equaliser.

But the appearance of Mick Harford for Goodman proved decisive. Barton headed on a Leonhardsen cross and the substitute, as early as the 35th minute, nodded home the winner. It would have been 4-2 if Pavel Srnicek, blatantly moving before the kick, had not saved Barton's late penalty.

Jones declared: "We knew Newcastle were good going forward. We talked about them during the week, but then we thought, 'Sod it, let them worry about us'."

## League Table After Match

| | P | W | D | L | F | A | Pts |
|---|---|---|---|---|---|---|---|
| Man Utd | 15 | 11 | 1 | 3 | 31 | 10 | 34 |
| Blackburn | 15 | 10 | 3 | 2 | 31 | 13 | 33 |
| Newcastle | 15 | 10 | 3 | 2 | 33 | 16 | 33 |
| Liverpool | 14 | 9 | 2 | 3 | 32 | 14 | 29 |
| Nottm Forest | 15 | 8 | 4 | 3 | 25 | 15 | 28 |
| Leeds | 15 | 7 | 3 | 5 | 23 | 19 | 24 |
| Chelsea | 14 | 7 | 2 | 5 | 25 | 19 | 23 |
| Man City | 15 | 6 | 4 | 5 | 25 | 25 | 22 |
| Norwich | 15 | 5 | 6 | 4 | 13 | 13 | 21 |
| Southampton | 15 | 5 | 5 | 5 | 23 | 26 | 20 |
| Arsenal | 14 | 5 | 4 | 5 | 17 | 14 | 19 |
| C Palace | 15 | 5 | 4 | 6 | 15 | 18 | 19 |
| Coventry | 15 | 5 | 4 | 6 | 18 | 26 | 19 |
| Wimbledon | 15 | 5 | 3 | 7 | 17 | 26 | 18 |
| Tottenham | 14 | 5 | 2 | 7 | 24 | 30 | 17 |
| Sheff Wed | 15 | 4 | 5 | 6 | 16 | 22 | 17 |
| West Ham | 15 | 5 | 2 | 8 | 9 | 16 | 17 |
| QPR | 15 | 4 | 4 | 7 | 23 | 27 | 16 |
| Aston Villa | 15 | 3 | 4 | 8 | 19 | 27 | 13 |
| Ipswich | 15 | 3 | 1 | 11 | 14 | 30 | 10 |
| Leicester | 14 | 2 | 3 | 9 | 14 | 26 | 9 |
| Everton | 14 | 1 | 5 | 8 | 9 | 24 | 8 |

# *November 26*

---

**NEWCASTLE 1**

**IPSWICH 1**

*(Half-time score : 0-0)*

*Newcastle:* Srnicek, Hottiger, Beresford, Venison, Neilson, Albert (Clark 45), Fox, Watson, Cole, Beardsley, Lee (Mathie 61).
*Sub:* Hooper.
*Ipswich:* Forrest, Yallop, Youds, Linighan, Whelan, Thomsen, Williams, Sedgley, Mason, Marshall (Slater 15), Paz.
*Scorers:* (Newcastle): Cole 86; (Ipswich): Thomsen 89.
*Referee:* K Cooper (Pontypridd).
*Attendance:* 34,459

With Andy Cole back in goal-scoring business one would think Kevin Keegan would be doing handstands at Newcastle. Instead the manager's face as the striker returned from injury was a mask of disappointment.

For a start he was concerned about injuries to two more of his internationals. Robert Lee and Belgian Philippe Albert, both crucial to United's trophy-winning quest, will miss Wednesday's Coca-Cola Cup tie at Manchester City and several games beyond.

But Keegan was also clearly disappointed with the way Ipswich seemed to consider entertaining play a crime. The manager, normally a good loser, was not quite sure what rankled more, Ipswich's negative ways or the inability of his would-be champions to hold a winning lead for three, short, final minutes.

"That was our naivety, a throwback to Bilbao in the Uefa Cup, and probably why we are not yet ready to win something major," he said. "It was just like Bilbao, 3-0 up in the first leg, the tie finished and with Liverpool it would be. Newcastle? We throw it back into the fire. That's when we look like a team who have come a long way in a short time."

But there was just as much disdain in his voice for Ipswich and the way they strangled the life out of this game and Newcastle's bid to join Blackburn in overtaking Manchester United. "For me to have to watch a team play the way they tried to play is dead against everything I stand for, "Keegan said.

"I was surprised Ipswich came here and played like that when I look at the people they have in charge. I've got a lot of respect for John Lyall. It was one of the most frustrating 90 minutes I've had to endure."

Not that Ipswich, who lost striker Ian Marshall with a fractured elbow, even dreamed of tendering apologies as they sloped off with a point secured by Claus Thomsen's 90th-minute equaliser.

Coach Paul Goddard, a former Newcastle striker, said: "Yes, we could have come here and attacked . . . and been done five or six."

"They can say what they want about the way we played, but we need the points," said Thomsen, the former Danish Under-21 star.

"The fact that we got one justifies the way we played." The argument would have been academic if Newcastle had made the most of Cole's 15th goal of the season, scored after 87 minutes. And, despite penning Ipswich in their own half for virtually the whole game, they failed to attack them down the flanks as often as they should.

*Andy Cole leaps above Paul Mason.*

# *November 30*

---

## MANCHESTER CITY 1
## NEWCASTLE 1

*(Half-time score : 0-1)*

*City:* Coton, Hill (Rosler 34),
D. Brightwell, Curle, I. Brightwell,
Summerbee, Lomas, Walsh,
Quinn, Flitcroft, Beagrie.
*Newcastle:* Srnicek, Hottiger,
Beresford, Venison, Neilson,
Watson, Clark, Jeffrey,
Beardsley, Cole, Mathie.
*Subs:* Hooper, Drysdale,
Holland.
*Scorers:* (City): Rosler 69;
(Newcastle): Jeffrey 11.
*Referee:* J Worrall (Warrington).
*Attendance:* 25,162

Kevin Keegan paid handsome tribute to 33-year-old Peter Beardsley after this storming Coca-Cola Cup tie, describing his performance as "the best I've ever seen from him".

Keegan added: "Peter was unbelievable. Others played well but he ran the show. He has a football brain but, more important, he retains a marvellous enthusiasm. Managers should send their young players out to watch him. Peter goes around as though he is a youngster on trial trying to impress."

Keegan had handed practically a full side over to his medical staff before the match but it gave him the chance to show Maine Road the quality of his Tyneside squad. Not even a full-scale bout of fisticuffs between Andy Cole and City captain Keith Curle could bruise the morale of a team bereft of eight seniors.

Newcastle had baptised a rousing fourth-round tie after 11 minutes with a first club goal from Mike Jeffrey. But even as last season's £60,000 recruit from Doncaster crashed the ball in, Keegan noted it all started from Beardsley. The little England maestro was in one of those moods. His brilliant ball to the flank was returned into the box by Lee Clark and Alan Neilson's header was met emphatically by Jeffrey's left foot.

City were shocked and entitled to be as Beardsley shredded their nerves and defence with a stunning array of passes. City manager Brian Horton was forced to rejig as full back Andy Hill hobbled off with an injury in the 34th minute. German striker Uwe Rosler joined Niall Quinn up front and midfielder Steve Lomas reverted to defence to challenge Newcastle.

Cole, back in the side after a month out with shin splints, might easily have won the tie. The striker chipped one first-half effort from 20 yards against the bar. But the pace and virtuosity of Newcastle's play was punctuated four minutes before the break by an amazing confrontation between Cole and Curle. The City centre-back had applied a half-Nelson to his opponent as he contested possession and Tyneside's 15-goal terror responded by swinging a fist at Curle. Referee Joe Worrall could well have given the pair their marching orders but contented himself with brandishing yellow cards in their faces.

City took a firmer grip on the tie in the second half and in the 69th minute Quinn's flick on from Peter Beagrie's corner brought the equaliser from Rosler. The German bravely dived for a header that brought his sixth goal in nine outings and had City fans in the sold-out 25,162 gate chanting his name.

Cole, who threatened to turn City inside out at times, could easily have ended an eventful night with the winner. He chipped a brilliant effort above Andy Dibble from 20 yards which twanged City's bar. And in a heart-stopping finale he twice blazed wide with Dibble's goal at his mercy.

Horton admitted: "Newcastle had to make a lot of changes and their lads worked their socks off. But we also had our chances in a great game."

*Andy Cole grabs Keith Curle's shorts and takes a swing at him.*

# *December 3*

TOTTENHAM 4

NEWCASTLE 2

*(Half-time score : 2-2)*

*Tottenham:* Walker, Austin, Popescu, Calderwood, Mabbutt, Barmby, Anderton (Edinburgh 81), Sheringham, Howells, Klinsmann, Campbell.
*Newcastle:* Srnicek, Venison, Beresford, Fox, Beardsley, Cole, Clark, Hottiger, Mathie, Watson, Neilson.
*Subs:* Drysdale, Jeffrey, Hooper
*Scorers:* (Tottenham): Sheringham 15,39,71, Popescu 80; (Newcastle): Fox 30, 42.
*Referee:* D Gallagher (Banbury).
*Attendance:* 28,002

Gerry Francis trudges away from a game or a training pitch with the same head-bowed shuffle of a man deep in thought. This was no exception.

Tottenham's new manager had earlier been asked to explain how he had transformed the side – cured it of its kamikaze approach. The players were, after all, the same men whose indiscipline had forced his predecessor Ossie Ardiles to wrap up his romantic notions in his P45 and hit the road.

Well, Francis is no Mills and Boon reader. He is into heavier stuff. You do not play off the cuff with his scripts. He is also not a man to reach for bouquets – as he might have done after sending Tottenham fans home happy and cutting Newcastle four points adrift of the Premiership leaders. It was, moreover, a match to savour. A Teddy Sheringham hat-trick, a delightful late contribution from Gica Popescu and two from Ruel Fox had adorned a minor classic.

"You have to talk about a team defensively and a team offensively," said Francis. "It is a team game. Everyone has to know where they should be and all good players can play together.

"It will be at least a month before you see real results. And nothing was ever won without hard work, rolling up your sleeves. I know what I want. I don't know whether I'm hard but I suppose I am a hard task master. Nothing comes easy."

It could have been Kevin Keegan talking. Keegan himself had paused before boarding Newcastle's team coach, turned and offered an opinion that most share outside Lancashire. "I hope the championship doesn't become a two-horse race – and, no, don't write us off for the championship."

Keegan, on the evidence of the afternoon, was not even going to dismiss the possibility of Tottenham making a late challenge. "I just hope whoever does win the Premiership does it the right way. I'm sure they will. I happen to think Premiership football is a class act."

It was in this match. The skill, subtlety and pace matched any continental offering – and edged it with the added ingredient of traditional passion.

Tottenham took the points but, as the old cliché goes, football was

# Strike Happy!

**Above** Let the celebrations begin! Goal King Cole gets the season off to a flier as he celebrates another stunning goal with the adoring Toon Army.

**Right** Kevin Keegan shows off Paul Kitson, his new £2.5 million signing from Derby County.

# Glory Boys

**Above** Marc Hottiger congratulates Robert Lee after his goal against Coventry.

**Right** In Newcastle's first foray into Europe for 17 years, it was poor Royal Antwerp who were to suffer, with Newcastle winning 10-2 on aggregate. Here Robert Lee gets the better of Rudo Schmidts.

**Opposite page (top)** It's that man again! Lee takes the acclaim after his strike against Aston Villa.

**Opposite page (bottom)** Beardsley, the man who makes United tick, squeezes through against a wall of Blackburn Rovers defenders.

# Autumn Lights

**Right** They just get better and better … Beardley's stunning strike against Crystal Palace in October.

**Below** A party too early? Newcastle players mob Ruel Fox after his goal against Bilbao in the Uefa Cup.

**Opposite page (top)** Goals, goals, goals … Steve Watson scores against Sheffield Wednesday.

**Opposite page (bottom)** Peter Beardsley scores with an overhead kick against Queen's Park Rangers.

# Battling On

**Above**  Party time against Wimbledon in November.

**Right**  Vinny Jones earns his first yellow card of the season for this robust challenge on Robert Lee.

**Opposite (top)**  The man who proved Keegan wrong: the impressive Srnicek commanding his defence during the draw with Coventry in December.

**Opposite (bottom)**  Terry McDermott with Newcastle 'bargain buy' Keith Gillespie in the New Year.

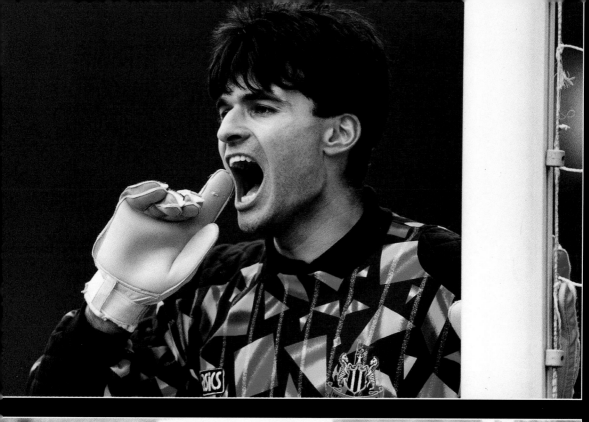

# Striking Magpies

**Right**  Rob Lee after scoring against Blackburn.

**Below**  Paul Kitson grabs a goal against fellow title challengers Manchester United in January.

# Local Hero

**Above** Lee Clark joins in the celebrations…

**Left** … And then provides some of his own.

# New Boy, Old Boy

**Opposite** Paul Kitson grabs his first in the FA Cup victory over Swansea.

**Above** Beardsley strikes against Aston Villa.

**Right** Beardsley lets fly against Arsenal. "He could play until he's 50," said manager Keegan of the ageless striker.

# Pride of the Tyne

Opposite (top) Keith Gillespie, the man who eased the pain of Cole's departure, scores his 'sitter' against Manchester City.

Opposite (bottom) Paul Kitson in a tussle with Southampton's Dodd in March.

Right Ruel Fox was one of Kevin Keegan's most inspired signings: Kevin was convinced that Fox could make it as a goalscorer and the former Norwich star proved the boss right on countless occasions this season. Here he celebrates another strike against Nottingham Forest in February.

Right Newcastle chairman Sir John Hall thought that Kevin Keegan was barmy to sign 31-year-old Beardsley. But he admits he has been won over by the strikers crucial and often spectacular goals. Here Beardsley scores what many regard as a contender for 'Goal of the Season': his spectacular second against Villa in February.

# Spring Troubles

**Above** Collymore breaks away for Forest against the Magpies. A goal looks certain, but Pavel Srnicek manages somehow to tip the ball away.

**Right** Lee Clark in a celebratory mood.

**Opposite** Ruel Fox after scoring against Nottingham Forest.

# Destroyers

**Opposite (top and bottom)** Alan Shearer did as much to damage United's title surge as anybody. Here, his headed goal against the Magpies during the VE weekend celebrations was vital for Blackburn's eventual title win.

**Left** Klinsmann strikes a crucial penalty home against Newcastle.

**Below** Klinsmann celebrates another as Peacock and Srnicek look disconsolate.

# Dual personality

**Opposite** John Burridge, Newcastle's goalkeeping coach, made history when he turned out against the club for Manchester City at the age of 43.

**Above** Peacock tussles with Collymore of Nottingham Forest.

**Left** Kitson hammers it home against QPR.

# Goodbye to Goal King Cole

**Opposite** Cole and Barnes, two of the finest black players to have graced English football.

**Left** Andy Cole in action against Chelsea.

**Below** R-E-S-P-E-C-T.

# Police ban Cole from Newcastle

'It would only add fuel to the flames'

**By JOHN BEAN**

ANDY COLE has been banned from returning to an emotive St James' Park tomorrow at the request of Newcastle Police.

They felt that the reappearance even as a spectator of the former Tyneside cult figure five days after his £7 million move to Manchester United could provoke crowd problems.

Cole, who limbered up in front of more than 1,000 spectators at United's training camp yesterday, had already been ruled out of playing in the match but the nation's most expensive attacker wanted to accompany United to their televised Premiership crunch match.

Old Trafford boss Alex Ferguson was ready to take him, until Newcastle contacted United at the police's request to ask that Cole be left behind.

"I would have been happy to take Andy and he would have liked to have gone to the match but I feel it would only add fuel to the flames," said Ferguson.

will stay away and watch the match on TV.

"In a year's time it will all have died down up there, Newcastle may be top of the league and that will take the pressure off us all."

### Compromise

Cole's Tyneside ban means Mark Hughes is set for a last hurrah in a Manchester United shirt as Everton line up a £2.25m compromise deal for the Welsh star next week.

Ferguson insists the speculation surrounding the future of one of the club's cult figures of the last decade will not affect Hughes one bit.

"Mark is a United player

Roache, is actively seeking a new club for the player.

"There is absolutely no problem with Mark playing at Newcastle on Sunday. He is a born winner and bursting to play.

"He is not the type to let all the speculation affect him. I would like to keep all my players but it's very difficult. You simply can't keep them all.

"His tremendous service over the years here means he doesn't deserve to miss the such a big match.

"He is strong mentally, as well as physically. As long as he is a United player it would be an insult to leave him on one side."

Andrei Kanchelskis, who has missed the last three games with a stomach strain

# Explain That!

**Opposite, top**  Happy days … Andy Cole and Ruel Fox celebrate a goal against Bilbao in the Uefa Cup.

**Opposite, bottom**  Cole beats Kharine and Johnsen to score against Chelsea.

**Above**  Kevin Keegan argues his case with angry fans outside St James' Park after the transfer of Cole to Manchester United.

**Right**  On police advice, Cole was left at home when Manchester United visited Newcastle the week after the transfer saga.

# Hope for the Future

**Left**  Keith Gillespie juggles the ball past Ian Nolan of Sheffield Wednesday.

**Below**  So Cole's gone; but as long as there's youngsters of the calibre of Keith Gillespie around, Newcastle will be challenging for honours for many years to come.

the winner. "It's better for the game if three or four clubs are challenging for the title," continued Keegan. "We don't want to see just
Manchester United and Blackburn up there battling it out together.
No one wants a situation which they've had in Italy or Spain where
one or two sides run away with it."

It is a worry for Keegan that his Geordie boys might contribute
much to English football but win little. "There is a danger of us always
entertaining but missing out on trophies, becoming a West Ham, a
standing joke," he said.

Jurgen Klinsmann, who garnishes lavish skill with commitment,
and Darren Anderton, belying his gangling appearance with such deft
touches, were conspirators in Newcastle's eventual downfall.
Sheringham scored two first-half goals with clinical finishes.

Both chances were provided by Anderton: a superb through ball
and an expert corner.

Each was followed by a Ruel Fox strike – one a glancing header, the
other after a deflected Lee Clark shot had hit the post. So it was even-
ly poised until 20 minutes from the end when an enchanting move
gave Sheringham his third.

Klinsmann's run from right to left was the springboard,
Sheringham's first-time crossfield pass to Dean Austin defence-split-
ting. As the ball sped into the penalty area Pavel Srnicek managed to
parry Klinsmann's diving header but Sheringham was on hand again.

Sheringham then linked with Popescu in a one-two which gave the
Romanian the opportunity of a punchline. And even then Klinsmann
might have added two more.

### League Table After Match

|  | P | W | D | L | F | A | Pts |
|---|---|---|---|---|---|---|---|
| Blackburn | 17 | 12 | 3 | 2 | 38 | 13 | 39 |
| Man Utd | 17 | 12 | 2 | 3 | 32 | 10 | 38 |
| Newcastle | 17 | 10 | 4 | 3 | 36 | 21 | 34 |
| Liverpool | 17 | 9 | 4 | 4 | 34 | 18 | 31 |
| Nottm Forest | 17 | 8 | 5 | 4 | 27 | 18 | 29 |
| Man City | 17 | 8 | 4 | 5 | 29 | 26 | 28 |
| Chelsea | 17 | 8 | 3 | 6 | 26 | 20 | 27 |
| Leeds | 16 | 8 | 3 | 5 | 24 | 19 | 27 |
| Norwich | 17 | 6 | 6 | 5 | 15 | 15 | 24 |
| Coventry | 17 | 6 | 5 | 6 | 20 | 27 | 23 |
| Tottenham | 17 | 6 | 4 | 7 | 29 | 33 | 22 |
| Arsenal | 17 | 5 | 6 | 6 | 20 | 18 | 21 |
| Southampton | 17 | 5 | 6 | 6 | 23 | 27 | 21 |
| Sheff Wed | 17 | 5 | 6 | 6 | 18 | 23 | 21 |
| C Palace | 17 | 5 | 5 | 7 | 15 | 19 | 20 |
| QPR | 17 | 5 | 4 | 8 | 25 | 32 | 19 |
| Wimbledon | 17 | 5 | 3 | 9 | 17 | 31 | 18 |
| West Ham | 17 | 5 | 2 | 10 | 10 | 19 | 17 |
| Aston Villa | 17 | 3 | 6 | 8 | 21 | 29 | 15 |
| Everton | 16 | 3 | 5 | 8 | 12 | 24 | 14 |
| Leicester | 17 | 3 | 4 | 10 | 18 | 30 | 13 |
| Ipswich | 17 | 3 | 2 | 12 | 16 | 33 | 11 |

# *December 10*

**NEWCASTLE 3**

**LEICESTER 1**

*(Half-time score : 1-0)*

*Newcastle:* Srnicek, Hottiger, Beresford, Venison, Peacock, Howey, Albert, Beardsley, Cole, Watson, Fox.
*Subs:* Clark, Mathie, Hooper.
*Leicester:* Poole, Blake, Whitlow, Thompson, Mohan, Hill, Grayson (Carr 79), Draper, Oldfield, Gee (Joachim 57), Philpott.
*Scorers:* (Newcastle): Albert 32, Howey 50, 70; (Leicester): Oldfield 48.
*Referee:* G Willard (Worthing).
*Attendance:* 34,400

Philippe Albert helped Newcastle take out some title-chasing insurance and then pledged his future to Kevin Keegan's side. Far from having his head turned by being linked with Barcelona, the Belgian defender is keen to stay at St James' Park beyond the year 2000.

Albert, a £2.7 million summer signing from Anderlecht, is not impressed that in some Spanish eyes he is seen as a likely successor to Ronald Koeman. "Twelve months ago that might have seemed like an appealing idea," he said, "but not now. I've probably got six or seven years left in me and if possible I'd like to play them here. I'd be happy if it was for the rest of my career.

"Kevin Keegan has signed for 10 years at Newcastle. If it's good enough for him, it would be good enough for me."

Keegan might just take him up on that idea, particularly if Newcastle were to overhaul Blackburn and Manchester United in the race for the Premiership title.

Even a manager who thrives on a daily diet of optimism would not have dared to suggest such a thought had his third-placed side fluffed this one. But, having secured victory over managerless Leicester, Newcastle are still very much in touch.

And it was little wonder Keegan described this as their most important win of the season. Defeat, or even the draw which at one stage struggling Leicester threatened to grab, would have just about damned them. It would have also wrecked the players' Saturday night Christmas party.

So it was as well that Albert's professed love affair with Newcastle is for real. With three first-class centre-halves in the club and only two berths to fill, Keegan asked Albert to play at left-back position he last tried seven years ago. "I decided to ring him up in the morning at home because he's bigger than me," said Keegan.

Albert did not get the huff. Instead he took it out on Leicester, producing his first two-goal performance in senior football.

Newcastle needed it in on a day when the game plan conceived by stand-in bosses Tony McAndrew and Kevin McDonald almost came off. McAndrew's strategy had been to deny Newcastle the possession required to fuel their normal passing game. And though the home side did score first through Albert, David Oldfield fired against the angle before heading a deserved equaliser.

In the end Mark Draper's efforts to induce a winning display from Leicester did not quite materialise as Steve Howey hit them with a second goal and Albert added another.

*Philippe Albert smashes in the first goal.*

# *December 17*

---

COVENTRY 0
NEWCASTLE 0

*(Half-time score : 0-0)*

*Coventry:* Ogrizovic, Borrows, Morgan, Pressley, Busst, Darby, Cook, Flynn, Wegerle (Boland 86), Ndlovu, Jones.
*Newcastle:* Srnicek, Beresford, Hottiger, Howey, Peacock, Venison, Kitson, Fox, Beardsley (Clark 56), Cole, Watson.
*Subs:* Bracewell, Hooper.
*Referee:* P Danson (Leicestershire).
*Attendance:* 17,233

Andy Cole's penalty failure raised a worrying question mark over Newcastle's championship credentials. It was not the mathematics of the miss which worried manager Kevin Keegan – two points lost now on Blackburn and Manchester United can be regained – so much as the unwillingness of his 'star players' to be put on the spot.

With Newcastle's regular penalty-taker Peter Beardsley off injured with a hamstring strain which may sideline him for a month, no one wanted to know when the penalty was awarded in the 85th minute. Keegan sat on the bench looking incredulous as his players shrugged their shoulders and refused to accept responsibility.

"I thought at one stage I might have to take it myself," he said. "What I wanted to see was players fighting over who would have the penalty. I was struggling to see anyone in my side play well and that was highlighted as players retreated when we got the spot-kick.

"I know how it is with penalties. A lot of people do not like to take them. So credit to Andy Cole. At least he had the guts to have a go."

Cole is one of the country's most prolific goal-scorers, but he had never taken a big-time penalty before. "I am not a penalty-taker but no one else wanted to," he said. "If it goes in you are a hero but I missed."

It seems extraordinary in these days when professional footballers earn fortunes, and when penalty shoot-outs can mean so much, that a team of Newcastle's standing were reduced to such fearfulness by a spot-kick. Cole's effort was awful. He put the ball down sheepishly, walked a few paces away with his back to goal, turned, and ran up instantly to shoot. It came as no surprise when Steve Ogrizovic saved with ease.

Some will argue that penalty-takers are a singular breed, those like Eric Cantona, Matt Le Tissier and Ian Wright who are blessed with composure and an almost cock-sure certainty they will score. They will say Newcastle were just unlucky Beardsley had been forced off. But surely that is not good enough. Penalties are something players can work on in training, a specific part of their job in which they can improve themselves.

It would not have guaranteed a goal in Saturday's situation but it would certainly not have seen Newcastle so embarrassed by events here. If players cannot cope with the tension of a penalty kick in this type of mid-season clash, what about the tension of end-of-season title deciders?

Keegan admitted victory would have flattered his side saying, "That was one of the least effective performances we have produced since I joined the club, and that includes the First Division days.

"We have been hit by a lot of niggling injuries but that is no excuse. I have money to spend but I am not going to. The players we have are good enough already. If I bought new people it would only upset the balance of the squad. We just have to keep on playing, keep faith and look forward to the return of the likes of Beardsley and Robert Lee."

Coventry might have won the game had Roy Wegerle or Peter Ndlovu accepted good chances. But that pair's skill, allied to tremendous teamwork and determination, should ensure a season without fear of relegation at Highfield Road.

Manager Phil Neal, who has worked impressively to create such stability, said: "A draw was probably fair. But that was only Wegerle's second match back from injury and he would usually have stuck his chance away."

## League Table After Match

|  | P | W | D | L | F | A | Pts |
|---|---|---|---|---|---|---|---|
| Blackburn | 19 | 13 | 4 | 2 | 41 | 15 | 43 |
| Man Utd | 19 | 13 | 2 | 4 | 36 | 14 | 41 |
| Newcastle | 19 | 11 | 5 | 3 | 39 | 22 | 38 |
| Nottm Forest | 19 | 10 | 5 | 4 | 33 | 20 | 35 |
| Liverpool | 18 | 9 | 5 | 4 | 34 | 18 | 32 |
| Leeds | 19 | 9 | 4 | 6 | 29 | 25 | 31 |
| Norwich | 19 | 8 | 6 | 5 | 19 | 15 | 30 |
| Man City | 19 | 8 | 4 | 7 | 30 | 31 | 28 |
| Chelsea | 18 | 8 | 3 | 7 | 26 | 23 | 27 |
| Tottenham | 19 | 7 | 5 | 7 | 32 | 34 | 26 |
| Arsenal | 19 | 6 | 6 | 7 | 23 | 22 | 24 |
| Coventry | 19 | 6 | 6 | 7 | 20 | 29 | 24 |
| QPR | 19 | 6 | 4 | 9 | 29 | 35 | 22 |
| Wimbledon | 19 | 6 | 4 | 9 | 21 | 33 | 22 |
| Southampton | 18 | 5 | 6 | 7 | 25 | 30 | 21 |
| C Palace | 19 | 5 | 6 | 8 | 15 | 20 | 21 |
| West Ham | 19 | 6 | 3 | 10 | 15 | 21 | 21 |
| Sheff Wed | 19 | 5 | 6 | 8 | 19 | 28 | 21 |
| Everton | 19 | 4 | 7 | 8 | 15 | 24 | 19 |
| Aston Villa | 18 | 3 | 7 | 8 | 21 | 29 | 16 |
| Leicester | 19 | 3 | 5 | 11 | 19 | 33 | 14 |
| Ipswich | 19 | 3 | 3 | 13 | 19 | 39 | 12 |

# *December 21*

**NEWCASTLE 0**

**MANCHESTER CITY 2**

*(Half-time score : 0-1)*

*Newcastle:* Srnicek, Hottiger (Bracewell 62), Beresford, Peacock, Albert, Venison, Fox, Watson, Clark, Cole, Kitson.
*Subs:* Neilson, Hooper.
*City:* Dibble, I. Brightwell, Foster, Lomas, Kernaghan (Vonk 90), Gaudino (Quinn 59), Summerbee, Walsh, Rosler, Flitcroft, Beagrie.
*Scorers:* Rosler 11, Walsh 80.
*Referee:* M Reed (Birmingham).
*Attendance:* 30,156

Newcastle slid out of the Coca-Cola Cup as Manchester City claimed a quarter-final place few would have predicted. City, in the grip of an injury crisis, turned up at St James' Park supposedly set up for the replay kill. Yet, thanks in the main to German striker Uwe Rosler, they walked away having clinched a quarter-final trip to Crystal Palace. Rosler, who pushed Newcastle into this fourth-round replay three weeks ago, turned out to be the man who also pushed them out.

He scored a goal that rocked Kevin Keegan's side, previously unbeaten at home this season, after 11 minutes. And, although Newcastle created chance after chance, their spirit was never quite intact after that. Ten minutes from time Paul Walsh hit them with a killer second.

City boss Brian Horton said: "That was the best performance in my time as manager. A lot of people had written off our chances but it was a magnificent team performance.

"Kevin Keegan was the first to say we deserved it and I think we did. I told you this was a good ground for me. I won promotion here with Brighton, and won here with Oxford. Given the circumstances, it was something quite special."

Even the players Horton was able to rustle up in the absence of seven regulars were not all 100 per cent fit. Indeed Walsh, who has been struggling with groin problems, was cleared to play only hours before kick-off. Rosler, the man City fans now idolise, underlined why the love affair blazes so strongly.

The striker was scarcely second favourite to win a Nicky Summerbee cross from the right. He was outnumbered two to one but showed the determination to get a touch ahead of Darren Peacock and Steve Watson, and before keeper Pavel Srnicek could react, Rosler pounced on his own knockdown and prodded City in front.

Newcastle fans could hardly believe it, Keegan's side having so comprehensively outplayed City in the first match before Rosler earned them a replay.

When Newcastle did get their game together Andy Dibble's response in goal was positive and he set the tone for an evening of spectacular action with an important tip-over from Peacock. Philippe Albert also had a fine chance when the ball fell to him unmarked eight yards out but his shot finished in the stand.

City had a bit of cup luck when Lee Clark's shot beat Dibble but John Foster, in his first game of the season, headed off the line. Andy Cole also went close twice within a minute but was denied by blocks by Foster and Alan Kernaghan.

After soaking up so much pressure City secured victory after Srnicek pushed out a Summerbee cross. Substitute Niall Quinn got the first bite before Walsh fired home from six yards.

Horton added: "They had plenty of chances and we needed a bit of luck but sometimes you know when it's your night. The spirit from all the players was tremendous."

Keegan said: "I think that mentally we are a bit dead at the moment. Only one team played it like a cup tie tonight and that was City."

*Andy Cole fails
to score and
United are out.*

# December 26

LEEDS 0

NEWCASTLE 0

*(Half-time score : 0-0)*

*Leeds:* Lukic, Kelly, Pemberton, Wetherall (Worthington 85), Dorigo, White, Palmer, McAllister, Speed, Whelan, Masinga (Strachan 68).
*Newcastle:* Srnicek, Venison, Howey, Albert, Beresford, Lee, Fox, Watson, Bracewell, Kitson, Cole.
*Subs:* Clark, Peacock, Hooper.
*Referee:* J Worrall (Warrington)
*Attendance:* 39,337

Andy Cole flew into a rage as the frustration of his six-match scoring drought spilled over into angry conflict. The man whose life is normally associated with goal-scoring, dallied briefly and dangerously with the notion that he might have prize-fighting qualities.

Had it not been for the swift intervention of two Leeds players, in two separate incidents involving home defender John Pemberton, Newcastle's top scorer might have suffered a late knock-out, even from lenient referee Joe Worrall.

Carlton Palmer had to dive in to restrain Cole when his tackle on Pemberton produced a flurry of fisticuffs. Even the final whistle failed to signal the end of the feud. Leeds keeper John Lukic was so concerned that Pemberton was about the revive it that he forced his teammate to a standstill, allowing an angry Cole to head for the tunnel flanked by Kevin Keegan.

But manager Keegan, who insists Newcastle are still in with a championship shout despite losing further ground here, joined with Leeds boss Howard Wilkinson in playing down the Cole-Pemberton flare-up.

Keegan, more than happy with the single point, said: "There's nothing wrong with showing a bit of feeling. I'd have been amazed if he'd been sent off. He might have been booked, but Joe Worrall is one of those referees who understands that football is sometimes played with fire in the belly.

"One lad is trying to mark last season's scoring sensation out of the game and the other is trying to score goals. Andy is working harder for less reward. But he's the sort who could get two hat-tricks and a brace in the next four games."

Just one goal would have been a godsend on a day Newcastle showed Leeds and the Premiership a sharper defensive edge. The inability of Leeds to blunt it led to a game of low grade appeal.

Newcastle launched one honest-to-goodness attempt to snatch a win which would have revitalised a side experiencing a mid-winter slump with one win from nine games. But a world-class save from Lukic put an end to those thoughts as he clawed the ball from a Steve Howey header as it zoomed towards the top left-hand corner.

Without complaint Wilkinson detected a change of emphasis in a Newcastle side noted for their willingness to play previously with gay abandon – and Keegan did not really dispute it. "Scrooge is about," he said, "and, yes, we were meaner. But this is a good point and don't write us off for the championship. Keep us in the back of your minds."

Leeds, before their second-biggest crowd of the season, increased the tempo in the second half. Palmer headed a corner against the bar and Phil Masinga wasted a good far-post opportunity.

Maybe it would have been more attractive had Worrall not ignored Paul Kitson's first-minute penalty appeal following a tackle by Pemberton. But, like the game, that claim did not really get off the ground.

### League Table After Match

|  | P | W | D | L | F | A | Pts |
|---|---|---|---|---|---|---|---|
| Blackburn | 20 | 14 | 4 | 2 | 44 | 16 | 46 |
| Man Utd | 21 | 14 | 3 | 4 | 40 | 17 | 45 |
| Newcastle | 20 | 11 | 6 | 3 | 39 | 22 | 39 |
| Liverpool | 21 | 11 | 6 | 4 | 38 | 19 | 39 |
| Nottm Forest | 21 | 11 | 6 | 4 | 34 | 20 | 39 |
| Leeds | 20 | 9 | 5 | 6 | 29 | 25 | 32 |
| Norwich | 21 | 8 | 6 | 7 | 19 | 18 | 30 |
| Tottenham | 21 | 8 | 6 | 7 | 34 | 34 | 30 |
| Arsenal | 21 | 7 | 7 | 7 | 25 | 22 | 28 |
| Chelsea | 21 | 8 | 4 | 9 | 28 | 29 | 28 |
| Man City | 21 | 8 | 4 | 9 | 31 | 36 | 28 |
| Wimbledon | 21 | 8 | 4 | 9 | 25 | 35 | 28 |
| Sheff Wed | 21 | 7 | 6 | 8 | 28 | 30 | 27 |
| Southampton | 21 | 6 | 7 | 8 | 31 | 36 | 25 |
| Coventry | 21 | 6 | 7 | 8 | 21 | 34 | 25 |
| QPR | 21 | 6 | 6 | 9 | 31 | 37 | 24 |
| C Palace | 21 | 5 | 8 | 8 | 15 | 20 | 23 |
| West Ham | 21 | 6 | 4 | 11 | 16 | 23 | 22 |
| Aston Villa | 21 | 4 | 8 | 9 | 25 | 31 | 20 |
| Everton | 20 | 4 | 7 | 9 | 16 | 28 | 19 |
| Leicester | 21 | 3 | 6 | 12 | 21 | 36 | 15 |
| Ipswich | 21 | 3 | 4 | 14 | 20 | 42 | 13 |

*Cole in yet another argument with John Pemberton.*

# December 31

**NORWICH 2**

**NEWCASTLE 1**

*(Half-time score : 2-1)*

*Norwich:* Marshall, Goss, Adams, Polston, Newsome, Sutch, Crook (Newman 75), Milligan, Ullathorne, Sheron (Cureton 59), Ward.
*Newcastle:* Srnicek, Venison, Beresford, Howey, Peacock, Watson (Clark 65), Bracewell, Lee, Fox, Cole, Kitson.
*Subs:* Hottiger, Hooper.
*Scorers:* (Norwich): Adams 1, Ward 10; (Newcastle): Fox 40 pen.
*Referee:* B H Hill (Wilbarston).
*Attendance:* 21,172

Norwich skipper Jon Newsome gingerly stemmed the flow of blood from his broken nose and backed Newcastle to maintain their title challenge to the end of the season. Kevin Keegan's view was that this outrageously unlucky defeat had scuppered any chance of the championship returning to the North-East this year. But Newsome, a title-winner with Leeds three years ago, was not convinced after a thrilling match in which his nasty injury occurred in a collision with Andy Cole. "Newcastle were simply brilliant," he said. "No other team has put us under so much pressure this season, including Blackburn and United.

"But our keeper [teenage debutant Andy Marshall] was magnificent and we held on when it was Alamo stuff at the end. I could have gone off but I was able to carry on breathing and it was wonderful to be part of such a victory.

"It helps us to keep on proving the critics wrong who wrote us off as relegation no-hopers at the start of the season. We are seventh in the table and still in both cups. A few clubs would like to be able to say that.

"No one should write off Newcastle either. They are a superb team and still have people like Peter Beardsley out injured."

The lustre was back in Newcastle's football on Saturday as they displayed the eagerness and enjoyment generated by Keegan, whose shining enthusiasm lights up a football scene so bedevilled by cynicism, corruption and double talk.

The *joie de vivre* is matched off the field and, when Keegan talks in a waterfall of words after games, his honesty and openness are always refreshing. But there was no need for him to be quite so keen to write off Newcastle's championship hopes.

"Our title aspirations have gone out of the window today," he said, "We'll keep fighting of course but we have lost too many matches against teams like Norwich that we shouldn't.

"To win the League you have to maintain consistency and we haven't done that. Neither Blackburn nor Manchester United have played as well as us in some games this season. But they haven't played as poorly as us either. Somewhere in the middle, like them, is what it takes to win championships."

This defeat left Newcastle 10 points adrift of Blackburn with exactly half the season played. That is not an impossible gap to close and as Keegan himself acknowledged, his team looked at last to have shaken off the lethargic form which has seen them win only one of their last 10 games.

They conceded two sucker-punch early goals to Norwich's Neil Adams and Ashley Ward inside 10 minutes, and then pounded the home side for the rest of the game.

Ruel Fox converted a penalty but Norwich's 19-year-old goalkeeper Marshall, on his full debut, made a string of inspired saves in siege conditions to leave the home fans with a tingle of delight from a special day.

Keegan said: "It was a fairy-tale for him and football needs those fairy-tale stories to retain its magic. I just wish it hadn't happened to us. We were creative and inventive and I couldn't fault the players' effort. My players have started to believe in their football again and that's something for us to hang on to."

That is the real reason Newcastle should not be discounted in the title race, despite Keegan's pessimism, which some might interpret as an attempt to take the pressure off his players.

When Cole and Co play with this passion and flair they can match anyone. John Beresford had a great game at left-back, hitting the post with one shot, and Fox was a box of tricks all afternoon, back to his elusive best.

The one area of the side needing attention is central defence. The marking was awful at times and if Belgian defender Philippe Albert's knee injury does mean him missing the rest of the season, Keegan should buy an international-class replacement.

Norwich were rock solid in defence, mainly due to a defensive outlook and playing for goals on the counter-attack. It is a year since club chairman Robert Chase was condemned for letting Mike Walker go in the wake of their European adventure, and six months since Chris Sutton was sold.

The cynics said Norwich would sink but Chase never ducked the critics or the criticism. And now he can afford a wry smile as their new £500,000 striker Ward has scored four goals in five games to keep the Norwich talent machine well-oiled and talk of crisis strictly reserved for elsewhere.

*Kitson goes down under Ullathorne's challenge.*

### League Table After Match

|  | P | W | D | L | F | A | Pts |
|---|---|---|---|---|---|---|---|
| Blackburn | 21 | 15 | 4 | 2 | 45 | 16 | 49 |
| Man Utd | 22 | 14 | 4 | 4 | 42 | 19 | 46 |
| Liverpool | 22 | 12 | 6 | 4 | 40 | 19 | 42 |
| Newcastle | 21 | 11 | 6 | 4 | 40 | 24 | 39 |
| Nottm Forest | 22 | 11 | 6 | 5 | 35 | 23 | 39 |
| Tottenham | 22 | 9 | 6 | 7 | 38 | 34 | 33 |
| Norwich | 22 | 9 | 6 | 7 | 21 | 19 | 33 |
| Leeds | 21 | 9 | 5 | 7 | 29 | 27 | 32 |
| Sheff Wed | 22 | 8 | 6 | 8 | 29 | 30 | 30 |
| Chelsea | 22 | 8 | 5 | 9 | 29 | 30 | 29 |
| Man City | 22 | 8 | 5 | 9 | 33 | 38 | 29 |
| Wimbledon | 22 | 8 | 5 | 9 | 26 | 36 | 29 |
| Arsenal | 22 | 7 | 7 | 8 | 26 | 25 | 28 |
| QPR | 22 | 7 | 6 | 9 | 34 | 38 | 27 |
| Southampton | 22 | 6 | 8 | 8 | 33 | 38 | 26 |
| West Ham | 22 | 7 | 4 | 11 | 19 | 24 | 25 |
| Coventry | 22 | 6 | 7 | 9 | 21 | 38 | 25 |
| C Palace | 22 | 5 | 8 | 9 | 15 | 21 | 23 |
| Everton | 21 | 5 | 7 | 9 | 20 | 29 | 22 |
| Aston Villa | 22 | 4 | 9 | 9 | 27 | 33 | 21 |
| Leicester | 22 | 3 | 6 | 13 | 21 | 37 | 15 |
| Ipswich | 22 | 3 | 4 | 15 | 21 | 46 | 13 |

# January 2

Ruel Fox fluffed a penalty chance to breathe new life into Newcastle's flagging championship challenge – and Kevin Keegan went berserk. The manager hit the roof, not because Fox made a hash of his 39th-minute spot-kick but because he took it in the first place.

"Don't ask me why Ruel Fox wanted to take it," said Keegan who expected skipper Peter Beardsley to be the man to put Stonewall City on the spot. When I saw Ruel put it down, I turned to Terry McDermott and said: 'I don't believe it'. If Ruel had wanted to take penalties he could have taken one down in Coventry when we needed volunteers. I went berserk at half-time."

When Fox, who scored with a penalty at Norwich the previous Saturday, made a mess of his latest effort, shooting tamely at Andy Dibble, it must have convinced City manager Brian Horton that it was going to be his day.

Horton employed the same tactics that brought him a Coca-Cola Cup quarter-final ticket against the odds, on the same ground two weeks ago. He played with three central defenders and, whenever necessary, packed his midfield to create a blue wall of frustration, and it worked.

"I'm not making any apology," Horton said, "I had no other choice because we were right down to the boards because of injuries. It was a bit negative. We set out our stall to defend because this was a game we couldn't afford to lose."

It was also a game Newcastle, with only one victory in 11 games desperately needed to win to convince their fans and themselves that the business of closing down the 12-point lead Blackburn have is not forlorn.

The penalty apart, the closest they came to cracking it was when a sliced Paul Bracewell shot beat Dibble but came back off the base of an upright. However, that close-run thing and the quality save Dibble made from a John Beresford header did not delude Keegan, who marked this down as a "very average performance".

Keegan sighed: "I didn't see many good things. They came to make it difficult for us and it worked. But we've known how to be good winners and have to accept it when things are not so good."

---

**NEWCASTLE 0**

**MANCHESTER CITY 0**

*(Half-time score : 0-0)*

*Newcastle:* Srnicek, Venison, Beresford, Bracewell, Howey, Peacock, Fox, Kitson, Cole, Beardsley, Lee.
*Subs:* Clark, Hottiger, Hooper.
*City:* Dibble, Lomas, Phelan, Vonk (Simpson 75), Kernaghan, Foster, Flitcroft, Summerbee, Beagrie, Walsh, Rosler.
*Referee:* A Wilkie (Chester le Street).
*Attendance:* 34,437

| | P | W | D | L | F | A | Pts |
|---|---|---|---|---|---|---|---|
| Blackburn........... | 22 | 16 | 4 | 2 | 49 | 18 | 52 |
| Man Utd............ | 23 | 15 | 4 | 4 | 44 | 19 | 49 |
| Liverpool......... | 23 | 13 | 6 | 4 | 44 | 19 | 45 |
| Nottm Forest.... | 23 | 12 | 6 | 5 | 36 | 23 | 42 |
| Newcastle......... | 22 | 11 | 7 | 4 | 40 | 24 | 40 |
| Tottenham......... | 23 | 10 | 6 | 7 | 39 | 34 | 36 |
| Leeds................. | 22 | 9 | 6 | 7 | 29 | 27 | 33 |
| Norwich............. | 23 | 9 | 6 | 8 | 21 | 23 | 33 |
| Wimbledon......... | 23 | 9 | 5 | 9 | 28 | 37 | 32 |
| Sheff Wed......... | 23 | 8 | 7 | 8 | 30 | 31 | 31 |
| Man City............ | 23 | 8 | 6 | 9 | 33 | 38 | 30 |
| Chelsea.............. | 22 | 8 | 5 | 9 | 29 | 30 | 29 |
| Arsenal............. | 23 | 7 | 7 | 9 | 26 | 26 | 28 |
| QPR..................... | 22 | 7 | 6 | 9 | 34 | 38 | 27 |
| Southampton..... | 23 | 6 | 9 | 8 | 34 | 39 | 27 |
| West Ham.......... | 23 | 7 | 4 | 12 | 21 | 28 | 25 |
| Coventry........... | 23 | 6 | 7 | 10 | 21 | 40 | 25 |
| C Palace............ | 23 | 5 | 8 | 10 | 15 | 22 | 23 |
| Aston Villa......... | 23 | 4 | 10 | 9 | 27 | 33 | 22 |
| Everton.............. | 22 | 5 | 7 | 10 | 21 | 31 | 22 |
| Ipswich.............. | 23 | 4 | 4 | 15 | 25 | 47 | 16 |
| Leicester............ | 23 | 3 | 6 | 14 | 22 | 41 | 15 |

Though it would have been a travesty considering the low level of their attacking input, City even have won it in the final quarter-hour. Pavel Srnicek made a super save to keep out a header from Michel Vonk, the man whose push on Darren Peacock gave Fox his penalty chance.

And twice late on City went close to repeating their Coca-Cola Cup success. Paul Walsh failed narrowly with an exquisite 20-yard chip. Then, right at the death, Peter Beagrie volleyed wide from eight yards when he might as have easily scored.

It made for a grey day for Newcastle whose leading scorer Andy Cole has now gone eight games without a goal.

*Cole commiserates with Fox after his penalty miss.*

# *January 8*

Robert Lee rediscovered his scoring touch yesterday just in time to hold up Blackburn's steady march towards double honours this season. After hitting 11 goals in the first 11 games of the season to win England recognition Lee had failed to find the target for Newcastle since October 1 and the fans shared his relief as the grim run ended at St James' Park.

Kenny Dalglish's Blackburn left Tyneside with what seemed like a legitimate grudge against referee Dermot Gallagher. He disallowed a goal apiece from Rovers' SAS squad Alan Shearer and Chris Sutton and, when he puts his feet up at home in Banbury to review his performance on video, he may have the grace to blush.

Though he was right to rule out Sutton's goal in the 20th minute for a push on Steve Howey, there is little doubt that the one from Shearer two minutes before the interval should have stood. Fifty per cent accuracy is not good enough.

In the game's dying moments he also failed to notice that Ruel Fox had been dragged back by his shirt after turning Paul Warhurst like a tailor's dummy.

Yet, despite sub-standard refereeing, a draw was probably the right result with Blackburn clearly in control of the game until they lost Stuart Ripley through injury just before the break. In that opening 45 minutes it was a matter of 'who dares wins' and those schooled in the art of counter-attacking could only admire Rovers.

There is a lot of nonsense talked about the quality of Blackburn's football. Here they put Kevin Keegan's side through the wringer and hung them out to dry. But when they lost Ripley's ability to bring the ball swiftly out of defence in the second half Newcastle assumed control.

They were doubtless encouraged during the interval by a few words from Keegan that would not have been heard at Evensong last night. There were even glimpses of the old Newcastle. Lee looked revitalised, Peter Beardsley was at last threading a few passes and Andy Cole seemed set to end his nine-game goal famine.

The crowd, who have suffered through a run of one victory in 12 games, responded and for a nostalgic half-hour they rediscovered the early-season mood.

## NEWCASTLE 1
## BLACKBURN 1
*(Half-time score : 0-1)*

*Newcastle:* Srnicek, Venison, Beresford, Peacock, Howey, Bracewell, Fox, Lee, Elliott (Kitson 72), Beardsley, Cole. *Subs:* Watson, Hooper.
*Blackburn:* Flowers, Berg, Le Saux, Hendry, Warhurst, Sherwood, Ripley (Newell 45), Atkins, Wilcox, Shearer, Sutton.
*Scorers:* (Newcastle): Lee 56; (Blackburn): Sutton 30.
*Referee:* D Gallagher (Banbury).
*Attendance:* 31,721

Yet Newcastle might have been a goal behind after 15 seconds. Ripley's pace took him beyond John Beresford but Pavel Srnicek saved at his near post.

The response from cunning Ruel Fox was instant. Graeme Le Saux hauled him down on the edge of the area and Barry Venison's ball in from a short free-kick should have been converted. Then Cole, exploding between Le Saux and Colin Hendry, might have toe-poked a long ball from Beresford past Tim Flowers but his effort inched just wide.

Rovers were getting passes in early to their 40-goal strike force and the ploy seemed to have worked in the 20th minute as Le Saux belted the ball forward. Sutton bulldozed past Steve Howey and Darren Peacock and blasted into the net but Gallagher had spotted a push and the goal was disallowed.

Undeterred, Sutton scored legally 10 minutes later. Cole and Lee had shots blocked by Hendry before Sutton and Shearer performed a neat one-two and Sutton clipped his 18th goal of the season past the hesitant Srnicek. Then Shearer netted from another Le Saux long ball only for the referee to confuse a shoulder-to-shoulder clash with a push and disallow a goal that should have stood.

Newcastle claimed the equaliser after 56 minutes Venison had driven a ferocious shot against the bar and Jason Wilcox headed out from Cole as United pressed. Shearer lost possession in trying to clear and Lee cut inside to strike a sweet shot inside Flowers' right-hand post from just outside the penalty area.

United closed in for the kill but Blackburn can defend as well and Hendry and Warhurst stood solid in face of the onslaught.

Paul Kitson, a 72nd-minute substitute, might have wrapped it up for Newcastle in the 89th minute but he headed Beardsley's fine cross over the bar. A winner then might have been less than Blackburn deserved for their contribution to an excellent cup tie. But at least Lee has recovered from his goal drought and that is a bonus for Tyneside.

*Steve Howey jumps on
Robert Lee who scored
in the 56th minute.*

# *January 15*

---

**NEWCASTLE 1**

**MANCHESTER UNITED 1**

*(Half-time score : 0-1)*

*Newcastle:* Srnicek, Venison, Beresford, Peacock, Howey, Elliott, Fox, Lee, Kitson, Hottiger, Clark.
*Subs:* Mathie, Watson, Hooper.
*United:* Schmeichel, Irwin, Bruce, Keane, Pallister, Cantona, Butt (May 45), McClair, Hughes (Scholes 15), Giggs, Sharpe.
*Scorers:* (Newcastle): Kitson 67; (Manchester): Hughes 13.
*Referee:* S Lodge (Barnsley).
*Attendance:* 34,471

There may be no Cole but the soul of Newcastle United lives on, embodied in the spirit of Paul Kitson. He stepped into the void left by the man who must now re-ignite Manchester United's title challenge. There was a cruel irony in the fact that Kitson's goal equalised one scored by Mark Hughes with what may well prove to be his last kick for the club he has served with such loyalty and dedication.

Hughes' 13th-minute strike may have been the postscript to a career which has never been less than charismatic. As he scored the boot of goalkeeper Pavel Srnicek sliced down the side of his knee like a surgeon's scalpel, inflicting ligament damage that had manager Alex Ferguson concerned about his immediate future.

Whatever the gut feeling of Newcastle's fans about the loss of Andy Cole – some have shown less sense of bereavement for the dearly beloved of their own families – they did not turn their grief on Kevin Keegan.

The depth of the support from the Toon Army for their manager was perhaps the most emotional aspect of an afternoon where the football was sometimes fretful.

If the manager had backing from the stands he had Trojan effort from his team, too, players prepared to spill their last beads of sweat and offer their last dregs of energy for the cause.

While that sense of duty prevails at Newcastle, and while Keegan maintains the profile of a Pied Piper, Sir John Hall need have no fears about his huge investments.

The loss of Hughes had a profound effect on the champions, their football becoming disjointed and fragile. Ferguson admitted his side were fortunate to escape this cauldron with a point and yet in the last exhausting minutes of the game Eric Cantona, of all people, squandered two chances to secure a victory Manchester United hardly deserved.

The champions could barely have begun with more encouragement than that provided by Hughes' goal. The Welshman went into the match knowing that the arrival of Cole might mean this was his last in a Manchester shirt. But there was no hint of anything other than complete concentration as Roy Keane crossed from the right and Hughes darted for the chance. As Srnicek ran towards him, Hughes stuck out his right foot to deliver the goal and in crunched the boot on his knee to cause the damage.

Newcastle would not pull back, however, and they probed to find the sensitive areas of United's defence, which responded by pushing forward to provide a surfeit of offside decisions.

Lee Clark, one of the rising young stars in Keegan's firmament, peppered Peter Schmeichel's goal to suggest that, if there are goalscoring vacancies, he wishes to post his claim for one of them.

Newcastle had two chances just before half-time, Steve Howey missing his kick from only 10 yards and Robert Lee sending another of Kitson's lay-offs skimming over the bar.

Keegan's side deserved some reward for their persistence and it came in the 67th minute as the probing Lee again got the ball into the Manchester area. This time Kitson got a lucky rebound off Gary Pallister and, as Schmeichel came off his line, he stuck the ball straight between his legs. It was a sweet goal for a man charged with an awful responsibility.

There were three promising chances for Manchester United in the last seven minutes, Keane just failing to thread the ball through Srnicek's legs and Cantona shooting wide with two shots he would usually expect to put away as a matter of habit.

## *League Table After Match*

|  | P | W | D | L | F | A | Pts |
|---|---|---|---|---|---|---|---|
| Blackburn | 23 | 17 | 4 | 2 | 52 | 18 | 55 |
| Man Utd | 24 | 15 | 5 | 4 | 45 | 20 | 50 |
| Liverpool | 24 | 13 | 6 | 5 | 44 | 20 | 45 |
| Nottm Forest | 24 | 12 | 6 | 6 | 36 | 26 | 42 |
| Newcastle | 23 | 11 | 8 | 4 | 41 | 25 | 41 |
| Tottenham | 24 | 11 | 6 | 7 | 41 | 35 | 39 |
| Wimbledon | 24 | 10 | 5 | 9 | 30 | 38 | 35 |
| Leeds | 23 | 9 | 7 | 7 | 29 | 27 | 34 |
| Norwich | 24 | 9 | 6 | 9 | 22 | 25 | 33 |
| Sheff Wed | 24 | 8 | 8 | 8 | 31 | 32 | 32 |
| Man City | 24 | 8 | 7 | 9 | 33 | 38 | 31 |
| Chelsea | 23 | 8 | 6 | 9 | 30 | 31 | 30 |
| Arsenal | 24 | 7 | 8 | 9 | 27 | 27 | 29 |
| Southampton | 24 | 6 | 10 | 8 | 34 | 39 | 28 |
| QPR | 23 | 7 | 6 | 10 | 35 | 40 | 27 |
| C Palace | 24 | 6 | 8 | 10 | 17 | 22 | 26 |
| Coventry | 24 | 6 | 8 | 10 | 21 | 40 | 26 |
| Aston Villa | 24 | 5 | 10 | 9 | 29 | 34 | 25 |
| West Ham | 24 | 7 | 4 | 13 | 22 | 30 | 25 |
| Everton | 23 | 5 | 8 | 10 | 22 | 32 | 23 |
| Ipswich | 24 | 5 | 4 | 15 | 26 | 47 | 19 |
| Leicester | 24 | 3 | 6 | 15 | 22 | 43 | 15 |

# *January 18*

---

### BLACKBURN 1
### NEWCASTLE 2

*(Half-time score : 0-0)*

***Blackburn:*** Flowers, Hendry, Le Saux, Shearer, Wilcox, Sutton, Slater (Wright 69), Berg, Atkins (Newell 87), Warhurst, Pearce.
***Newcastle:*** Srnicek, Venison, Beresford, Fox, Howey, Lee, Clark, Hottiger, Peacock, Elliott, Kitson.
***Subs:*** Bracewell, Watson, Hooper.
***Scorers:*** (Blackburn): Sutton 75; (Newcastle): Hottiger 58. Clark 85.
***Referee:*** D Gallagher (Banbury).
***Attendance:*** 22,658

Kevin Keegan hailed the relaunch of Newcastle's season after Lee Clark scored a stunning late winner to carry his team past the mighty FA Cup challenge of Blackburn Rovers.

"This will kick-start our season," said a jubilant Keegan. "This can get us back in the race for the title as well. There has been something a bit special about our performance."

The crucial second goal, five minutes from the end of a pulsating game, followed a build-up between Ruel Fox and Robert Lee. Clark received the ball at an angle on the right, turned and drove it superbly past Tim Flowers' near post.

Clark said: "All the lads have been ribbing me this week. They've been calling me jigsaw because they say I go to pieces in the box, but I did all right tonight." He revealed he was on a special fruit diet to improve his sharpness. "Some of the lads told me apples would be good for me, so I made sure I had a few and it seems to have worked."

Team-mate Barry Venison said: "He struck his goal beautifully. It gave us a huge lift."

Newcastle's Swiss international full-back Marc Hottiger had opened the scoring with a 25-yard free-kick that swerved so violently it moved from outside Flowers' right-hand post to just inside as the England keeper made a frantic dive. Hottiger, who has been left out because of poor form, struck the breakthrough goal with the outside of his right foot after Colin Hendry had been cautioned for a foul on Robbie Elliott. It made two missed first-half chances from Alan Shearer all the more costly.

Newcastle had come to Ewood Park in this third-round replay determined to attack, and Hottiger, bought for £600,000 by Keegan on the strength of his World Cup performances for Switzerland, could not hide his delight at getting the goal, his first for the club.

Rovers battled desperately to get on terms in the remaining half-hour and Hendry brought gasps of astonishment with an explosive 30-yard left-foot shot after a surging run from the half-way line.

Sutton finally made amends for Shearer when he drove home a 74th-minute equaliser after Paul Warhurst had headed down a Jason Wilcox centre. But Keegan's battlers struck again in the 85th minute through Clark's superb shot.

Rovers had begun well and might have been ahead in the first two minutes. A neat five-man move was rounded off with an unselfish pass from Wilcox for Sutton but he did not show the first touch of a £5.5 million striker and an excellent chance was wasted.

Then Graeme Le Saux, back after missing one match through injury, took a quick throw-in which enabled Wilcox to get beyond Hottiger. Darren Peacock's intervention looked clumsy but no penalty resulted.

It was a replay that was living up to Cup traditions and Blackburn were fortunate to survive when Steve Howey chipped a clever ball over the defence and Peacock, storming in behind them, headed across the face of goal and beyond the far post.

United were having their problems with Blackburn's 40-goal strike force of Shearer and Sutton and twice 23-goal Shearer got himself into scoring positions in the space of a few minutes. It was out of character that he should drive the first chance beyond the far post and put the second high after Sutton had laid on a superb chance from Warhurst's pass.

Newcastle fashioned a late, killing chance for Lee whose quick shot might have beaten any goalkeeper. But Flowers showed lightning reflexes to deflect the ball for a corner.

*Ruel Fox gets
past Le Saux.*

# *January 21*

SHEFFIELD WEDNESDAY 0
---
NEWCASTLE 0

*(Half-time score : 0-0)*

*Sheff Wed:* Woods, Atherton,
Nolan, Petrescu, Waddle,
Sheridan, Bart-Williams, Walker,
Ingesson, Whittingham, Watson
(Bright 58).
*Newcastle:* Srnicek, Venison,
Beresford, Fox, Howey, Lee
(Gillespie 45), Beardsley, Clark,
Hottiger, Peacock, Kitson.
*Subs:* Bracewell, Hooper.
*Referee:* R B Gifford
(Llanbradach).
*Attendance:* 31,215

Kevin Keegan flew off to try to buy himself a striker insisting that his interest in Chris Armstrong is dead. Only if Crystal Palace manager Alan Smith has second thoughts and accepts Keegan's £4.7 million bid will Armstrong have a chance of trekking up to Tyneside.

Meanwhile Newcastle boss Keegan headed for the Continent declaring that the real value-for-money deals are done on foreign soil these days. "I've got money to spend and might end up with two or three players. Only one will be from abroad because of the Europe player restriction on foreigners. When Philippe Albert is fit we'll have four on the books next season.

"Armstrong? We have put in a bid and it's been turned down. So it's finished as far as we're concerned."

Whatever happens on his European shopping trip the Newcastle boss believes he already has a player who could galvanise Geordie audiences for the next 10 years. Keith Gillespie pulled on the Magpies shirt here for the first time and in 45 minutes had shown the travelling Toon Army why Keegan tracked him for a year.

The Newcastle boss admitted after this rain-spattered stalemate he lacks a focal point for his attack after Andy Cole's £7 million departure to Old Trafford. But the slim, modestly built Gillespie, second-half substitute for the injured Robert Lee, showed enough pace and balance on the right flank to put the wind up the Wednesday bench on this gusty afternoon.

"I was glad the lad was sitting five yards away from me on the bench for the first 45 minutes rather than being out on the pitch," said Wednesday boss Trevor Francis.

Gillespie's arrival meant a re-jig of Newcastle's front line with £2.25 million Ruel Fox on the left and Peter Beardsley up front with Paul Kitson. That at least gave some much needed support to Kitson who had operated as a lone striker until then. Wednesday's Swedish midfield flank player Klas Ingesson went closest to carving victory from this wind-blasted bore in the 73rd minute, but Pavel Srnicek reacted brilliantly to foil him from three yards.

Gordon Watson, who had started up front for Wednesday in place of Mark Bright, made a gesture at his bench that looked suspiciously like a V sign when substituted in the 58th minute.

"He was frustrated about being taken off and wanted to go straight to the dressing room" said Francis. "But I think Gordon got the message we wanted him to stay in the dug-out and cool down. He did well in the first half. But I wanted to change the game at that stage and needed someone to keep possession a bit more." Keeper Chris Woods' first appearance since October, 1993, in place of the suspended Kevin Pressman reminded Wednesday fans of the quality that once made him England's No 1.

"I'll be disappointed if I'm not playing at West Ham on Monday but deep down I don't think I will be," he said." I've lost 15 months of my career and it's like starting out all over again. At least I hope I've given the manager a selection problem."

### League Table After Match

| | P | W | D | L | F | A | Pts |
|---|---|---|---|---|---|---|---|
| Blackburn | 24 | 17 | 4 | 3 | 52 | 19 | 55 |
| Man Utd | 25 | 16 | 5 | 4 | 46 | 20 | 53 |
| Liverpool | 24 | 13 | 6 | 5 | 44 | 20 | 45 |
| Newcastle | 24 | 11 | 9 | 4 | 41 | 25 | 42 |
| Nottm Forest | 25 | 12 | 6 | 7 | 37 | 28 | 42 |
| Tottenham | 24 | 11 | 6 | 7 | 41 | 35 | 39 |
| Wimbledon | 24 | 10 | 5 | 9 | 30 | 38 | 35 |
| Leeds | 23 | 9 | 7 | 7 | 29 | 27 | 34 |
| Sheff Wed | 25 | 8 | 9 | 8 | 31 | 32 | 33 |
| Norwich | 24 | 9 | 6 | 9 | 22 | 25 | 33 |
| Arsenal | 25 | 8 | 8 | 9 | 28 | 27 | 32 |
| Chelsea | 24 | 8 | 7 | 9 | 32 | 33 | 31 |
| Man City | 24 | 8 | 7 | 9 | 33 | 38 | 31 |
| Aston Villa | 25 | 6 | 10 | 9 | 31 | 35 | 28 |
| Southampton | 24 | 6 | 10 | 8 | 34 | 39 | 28 |
| QPR | 23 | 7 | 6 | 10 | 35 | 40 | 27 |
| C Palace | 25 | 6 | 8 | 11 | 18 | 25 | 26 |
| Everton | 24 | 6 | 8 | 10 | 25 | 33 | 26 |
| Coventry | 25 | 6 | 8 | 11 | 21 | 41 | 26 |
| West Ham | 24 | 7 | 4 | 13 | 22 | 30 | 25 |
| Ipswich | 25 | 5 | 5 | 15 | 28 | 49 | 20 |
| Leicester | 24 | 3 | 6 | 15 | 22 | 43 | 15 |

*Keith Gillespie juggles the ball past Ian Nolan.*

# *January 25*

---

NEWCASTLE 2
WIMBLEDON 1

*(Half-time score : 1-0)*

*Newcastle:* Srnicek, Venison, Hottiger, Elliott, Howey, Peacock, Bracewell, Fox, Gillespie, Beardsley, Kitson. *Subs:* Watson, Clark, Hooper
*Wimbledon:* Segers, Cunningham, Kimble (Elkins 45), Thorn, Perry, Jones, Goodman, Earle, Clarke (Blissett 77), Barton, Ekoku.
*Scorers:* (Newcastle): Fox 34, Kitson 51; (Wimbledon): Ekoku 78.
*Referee:* M Reed (Birmingham).
*Attendance:* 34,374

---

Ruel Fox came up with a wonderful strike but, like everyone else, still had to take a back seat to Irish whizz-kid Keith Gillespie. The 19-year-old winger, who arrived at St James' Park as the supposed makeweight in the £7m Andy Cole deal, illustrated spectacularly that he was not the type to settle for a bit part under Kevin Keegan.

Gillespie, valued at £1m in the deal, produced a storming home debut to set United on their way to a win that should have been more emphatic.

It was, of course, just as Keegan had predicted when he gambled by selling Cole. He forecast that Gillespie had the talent and temperament to persuade fans to embrace him as an instant favourite. And Gillespie duly took the match by the scruff of the neck and made it his own.

Gillespie handed out so much legitimate punishment to Wimbledon's Alan Kimble that the full-back did not reappear after half-time. Kimble did not seem injured and the chances are manager Joe Kinnear spared his demoralised defender further suffering. He replaced him with Gary Elkins as Wimbledon went in for a revamp that involved using skipper Vinnie Jones up front.

By that stage the Dons were a goal down and, almost surprisingly, Gillespie was not the scorer. It was Fox who crashed a superb, rising shot beyond Hans Segers.

Newcastle were well worth that lead against a side who tend to cause them problems; the Dons had won three of their last four games against Keegan's side. But six minutes into the second half Wimbledon's problems piled up. Paul Kitson took delivery of a leisurely pass from Barry Venison and clipped the ball over Segers to put United 2-0 ahead.

It was tough on Segers, whose unorthodox brilliance had kept Newcastle at bay earlier. But no one ever writes off Wimbledon and after 78 minutes Efan Ekoku underlined why. He got on the end of a Warren Barton free-kick and reduced the deficit.

There was controversy in the final seconds as Elkins forced in what looked like the equaliser. But eagle-eyed referee Mike Reed spotted an infringement, disallowed the goal and, predictably, there was a stormy protest from Wimbledon players.

An incensed Kinnear tried to take up his dispute with the referee and a policeman had to intervene as the official attempted to make his way down the tunnel.

Keegan said: "There didn't look much wrong with that goal, so maybe we've got to be thankful for small mercies. We played ever so well but squandered so many chances. We could have ended up with a point which would have been a travesty.

"As for Keith Gillespie, the crowd liked him and you can see what pace he has."

Kinnear said: "The referee is locked in his room. He has refused to talk. He won't even make any comment. They make decisions and they can't be punished. I knocked on his door and he told me to go away."

*Efan Ekoku after scoring in the 78th minute.*

# *January 28*

**NEWCASTLE 3**

**SWANSEA 0**

*(Half-time score : 1-0)*

*Newcastle:* Srnicek, Bracewell, Hottiger, Elliott, Howey, Peacock, Gillespie, Venison, Kitson, Beardsley, Fox.
*Subs:* Mathie, Watson, Hooper.
*Swansea:* Freestone, Jenkins, Walker, Basham, Ford, Chapple, Hayes (McFarlane 73), Penney, Torpey, Cornforth, Hodge.
*Scorers:* Kitson 41, 46, 72.
*Referee:* B Hill (Market Harborough).
*Attendance:* 34,372

Paul Kitson delivered Newcastle into the fifth round of the Cup but resisted the temptation to dash for the nearest post-box. The striker, whose hat-trick destroyed Swansea, has been the subject of some "hideous" letters from fans who do not think he can hold a candle to Andy Cole.

And after the Geordies continued their Cup charge, manager Kevin Keegan revealed: "I've had a few of them, basically saying he's just not a replacement for Andy. But he was never bought to do that.

"I've replied with a stock letter that thanks the writers for their comments and their interest in the club. But Paul Kitson has answered them more effectively than I could ever have done, and I think there may be a few people who might now be wondering whether they have judged him rashly.

"They have written some of the most hideous letters I have ever seen; obviously they think they know something about football."

Kitson would have needed to be living on another planet not to have picked up the vibes from Tynecastle fans, many of whom are still seething over the sale of their hero to Manchester United.

When Newcastle were returning by coach from Hillsborough after last weekend's goalless draw with Sheffield Wednesday, Keegan had to order the driver to switch off Radio 5 because of the criticism being levelled against his £2.25m striker. "There was a guy on there slaughtering him," Keegan said. "It was embarrassing and totally unfair."

It may explain why Kitson made a side-door exit from St James' Park on Saturday night, when a spectacular hat-trick – two headers and a delicate lob – entitled him to be out front milking the acclaim.

Though Swansea are Second Division, for almost half of this tie they did a magnificent job of making life difficult for one of the Premiership's most adventurous sides.

If one-time Arsenal winger Martin Hayes had not looked a gift-horse of a first-minute chance in the mouth, Keegan could well have been on the wrong end of the only real fourth-round upset. Until Kitson came up with the first of his classy treble just before half-time it looked as though this may have been Newcastle's swansong.

With skipper John Cornforth, the former Sunderland midfielder, an enormous influence, Frank Burrows' team, though ultimately out-played, did themselves proud.

Yet old pros like Burrows, who turns 51 today, know only too well that, when all is said and done, quality generally speaks a winning language. And while he gave Kitson his due, he knew he had been undone just as much, if not more, by the remarkable Peter Beardsley.

"The ability to make something out of nothing – that's what makes him such a super player," said Burrows, who in the late '60s super-vised a boot boy at Scunthorpe by the name of Kevin Keegan.

This time the boot was on the other foot. Newcastle had too much know-how, and the exceptional Paul Bracewell expressed much of it in midfield.

The good news for Kitson is that he is unlikely to be Newcastle's lone ranger for too much longer. Keegan said: "I think Andy Cole will score goals for Manchester United and we will score without him. But I'm now in a great position to get people to take this club forward. If Paul Kitson scores a hat-trick for the next five games, I shall still sign another striker, maybe two."

*Kitson scores his first with a header.*

# *February 1*

---

## NEWCASTLE 2
## EVERTON 0

*(Half-time score : 0-0)*

*Newcastle:* Hooper, Venison, Hottiger, Elliott (Clark 73), Neilson, Bracewell, Fox, Lee, Gillespie, Beardsley, Mathie.
*Subs:* Watson, Harper.
*Everton:* Southall, Jackson, Barrett, Unsworth, Watson, Horne, Ebbrell, Burrows (Samways 49), Limpar (Grant 64), Parkinson, Stuart.
*Scorers:* Bearsdley 80 pen, Fox 74
*Referee:* D Elleray (Harrow on the Hill).
*Attendance:* 34,465

It was a mad, mad night for Joe Royle and a bad, bad night for two of his players. On an occasion when pandemonium invaded the Premiership with a vengeance £1.7m new boy Earl Barrett and Barry Horne were dramatically sent off.

And, while there will be demands for referee David Elleray's head all over Merseyside this morning, at least one big name is ready to speak in his defence. Newcastle manager Kevin Keegan watched Elleray, the Harrow housemaster, book seven Everton players and three of his own as well as brandishing two red cards and backed him, declaring that rules are rules.

"Joe Royle is a good friend of mine," Keegan said, "but I think his team was very undisciplined tonight. I said at half-time to my players that if they keep this up they [Everton] could be down to 10 men. I did not realise how true those words would become.

"Some of them were asking to be booked. They had a lot of defenders and a lot of players in midfield and you have got to time your tackles properly Those are the rules."

There is no way that angry Royle is going to agree with that assessment of an issue which overshadowed almost every other aspect of this contest, but, rightly or wrongly, Everton have got themselves in big trouble in a season when their status in the top flight is in serious jeopardy.

It is a matter of opinion whether Elleray got his bookings right. It is a matter of fact that Newcastle struck the telling blows when it counted.

They came in the final-quarter hour when Ruel Fox and skipper Peter Beardsley scored the goals which pushed Newcastle into third place and Everton further into the mire.

Neville Southall, one of the players booked, hardly deserved such an outcome. He performed heroics in Everton's goal and, initially, was beaten only because of a mis-hit shot. Robert Lee's wonky volley wrong-footed Southall and allowed Fox to follow up and bury the rebound.

It was at that point that the Everton chairman Peter Johnson left the directors' box, creating the impression that he was signalling his disgust. He was followed by Sir Philip Carter, the club's former chairman. But it was later explained that there was no breech of directors' box decorum. Johnson had told Newcastle directors beforehand that he would be leaving early, no matter what the score.

In the context of a night full of bitterness it was easy to jump to conclusions but, if it was bad for Everton when Fox struck, it got seriously worse. David Unsworth tripped Beardsley in the box and the United skipper made sure of Newcastle's second from the penalty spot. Even that incident produced an unlikely booking. Southall was so disgusted with the award that, when Beardsley placed the ball on the spot, the veteran Welsh international marched up and kicked it off. As a result he became another victim of Elleray.

Royle argued that while they had 11 men on the pitch Everton were comfortable with their task, and he was right.

In fact they could have saved themselves a lot of trouble by tying the game up in the opening minutes when sanity was still in the air. But Swede Anders Limpar missed a glorious opportunity to send Everton on their way, failing to play in Graham Stuart when he would almost certainly have scored.

Royle said later: "The referee's display could have caused a riot. In 30 years in football it was the most insensitive refereeing display I've ever seen."

Maybe there was bound to be uncertainty in the air on a night when the dreaded 'flu bug all but laid Newcastle low. Saturday's Cup hero Paul Kitson, goalkeeper Pavel Srnicek and Darren Peacock failed to come out of the starting gate because of the virus. Srnicek's absence gave Mike Hooper his first senior outing for five months and only his second of the season.

Newcastle expect much these days from their teenage winger Keith Gillespie who broke powerfully from midfield to send Beardsley scampering away. But Southall did well to push away Beardsley's left-foot drive as the former Evertonian tried to kid the keeper on his near post.

In the midst of his team's renovations Royle gave the £1.7 million Barrett his debut at left-back. Barrett seemed determined to make his mark – and did when he dumped Newcastle full-back Marc Hottiger on the deck and was promptly booked for his trouble.

The Scot Alex Mathie was given his third start in the Premiership in place of Kitson and could have celebrated with a goal after half an hour. But Southall was up to that task as well as he tipped Mathie's looping header over the top from a Hottiger cross.

There have been mutterings from within about the state of Newcastle's pitch, particularly as it cost around £400,000 to lay in the summer. Certainly Mathie had cause to curse its condition as a mound of displaced turf cost him accuracy with a great shooting chance a few minutes after his header.

## League Table After Match

|  | P | W | D | L | F | A | Pts |
|---|---|---|---|---|---|---|---|
| Blackburn | 26 | 18 | 5 | 3 | 57 | 21 | 59 |
| Man Utd | 26 | 16 | 6 | 4 | 47 | 21 | 54 |
| Newcastle | 26 | 13 | 9 | 4 | 45 | 26 | 48 |
| Liverpool | 25 | 13 | 7 | 5 | 44 | 20 | 46 |
| Nottm Forest | 26 | 13 | 6 | 7 | 39 | 28 | 45 |
| Tottenham | 25 | 11 | 6 | 8 | 41 | 36 | 39 |
| Leeds | 25 | 10 | 8 | 7 | 34 | 28 | 38 |
| Sheff Wed | 26 | 9 | 9 | 8 | 33 | 32 | 36 |
| Wimbledon | 25 | 10 | 5 | 10 | 31 | 40 | 35 |
| Norwich | 25 | 9 | 7 | 9 | 24 | 27 | 34 |
| Arsenal | 26 | 8 | 9 | 9 | 29 | 28 | 33 |
| Aston Villa | 26 | 7 | 10 | 9 | 32 | 35 | 31 |
| Chelsea | 25 | 8 | 7 | 10 | 32 | 35 | 31 |
| Man City | 25 | 8 | 7 | 10 | 33 | 39 | 31 |
| Southampton | 25 | 6 | 11 | 8 | 35 | 40 | 29 |
| C Palace | 26 | 6 | 9 | 11 | 19 | 26 | 27 |
| QPR | 24 | 7 | 6 | 11 | 35 | 44 | 27 |
| Everton | 26 | 6 | 9 | 11 | 25 | 35 | 27 |
| Coventry | 26 | 6 | 9 | 11 | 23 | 43 | 27 |
| West Ham | 25 | 7 | 4 | 14 | 22 | 32 | 25 |
| Ipswich | 26 | 5 | 5 | 16 | 29 | 53 | 20 |
| Leicester | 25 | 4 | 6 | 15 | 23 | 43 | 18 |

# *February 4*

---

Terry Venables left QPR early ruminating about his England strike formation. There has been overwhelming evidence over the past two seasons about the value of performing a two-step, with partners like Cole and Beardsley, Cantona and Hughes, Sutton and Shearer setting the vogue.

Meanwhile England continue to have Shearer as an isolated striker. Venables vehemently claims his famed Christmas tree formation is evergreen. Yet at Loftus Road he had further evidence in the performance of Les Ferdinand and Kevin Gallen that there is much to be said for a pair of strikers playing in tandem.

Within seven minutes he had seen the devastating effect of that dual understanding with the teenage Gallen supplying and the experienced Ferdinand delivering. The game against flu-ravaged Newcastle was won there and then.

Sadly, the Cole-Beardsley combination has been broken-up. So to an extent, has the Cantona-Hughes axis. But what of the QPR pair? Can Rangers keep Ferdinand ?

"I'll certainly be doing my best," promises manager Ray Wilkins. "He's been quite exceptional since I came back here. He has worked his socks off. He enjoys playing football.

"I have to try and persuade him he can win things by staying with us. We have to wait and see. He is a London boy. He is 28. Does he want to leave London ? If he doesn't he has limited options.

"We would all be delighted if he stayed because not only is he a super footballer. He's a lovely lad as well and has the utmost respect among his peers."

Kevin Keegan, with £6m burning a hole in his pocket, must have been interested in Ferdinand's performance and he will not be alone in keeping a sharp eye on Gallen, a superb young prospect. Gallen has a strong physical presence, excellent awareness and the ability both to provide and to get in on the end of things, not dissimilar to Sutton.

"He is a good player, potentially exceptional," says Wilkins. "We are taking each step as it comes with him but he really is impressing me with each game he plays. The level of performance he manages to maintain is incredible for a 19-year-old. He has been so consistent and

---

**QPR 3**

**NEWCASTLE UNITED 0**

*(Half-time score : 3-0)*

**QPR:** Roberts, Bardsley, Maddix, Brevett, McDonald, Impey, Holloway, Barker, Ferdinand (Dichio 89), Gallen, Sinclair.
**Newcastle:** Hooper, Bracewell, Lee, Beardsley, Clark, Hottiger, Gillespie, Watson, Neilson, Elliott, Kitson (Mathie 52).
**Subs:** Drysdale, Harper.
**Scorers:** Ferdinand 4, 7, Barker 18.
**Referee:** K Cooper (Pontypriddd).
**Attendance:** 16,576

---

that has been a major asset for Les.

"In the past Les has had to do a bit too much but they are now complementing each other very nicely. It is two good footballers together realising they can rip people to pieces if they put their minds to it."

They were certainly too much for a makeshift United back unit with Marc Hottiger the only recognised player in position as a 'flu epidemic and a couple of suspensions knocked Keegan sideways.

He is not a man to seek excuses, however, and suggested: "I can take losing. But apart from losing most of our defence there were six other players who might have played.

"Anyway it took us 83 minutes to get a shot on goal and I would have expected us to create more problems than we did with the team we had out. The best thing for me about today was our fans.

"I still say that, when we have a team as good as our supporters, then we will really be worth something. We have made big strides and got a lot of good players. But today was a poor Newcastle performance."

## League Table After Match

| | P | W | D | L | F | A | Pts |
|---|---|---|---|---|---|---|---|
| Blackburn | 26 | 18 | 5 | 3 | 57 | 21 | 59 |
| Man Utd | 27 | 17 | 6 | 4 | 48 | 21 | 57 |
| Newcastle | 27 | 13 | 9 | 5 | 45 | 29 | 48 |
| Liverpool | 26 | 13 | 8 | 5 | 45 | 21 | 47 |
| Nottm Forest | 27 | 13 | 7 | 7 | 40 | 29 | 46 |
| Leeds | 26 | 10 | 9 | 7 | 34 | 28 | 39 |
| Tottenham | 25 | 11 | 6 | 8 | 41 | 36 | 39 |
| Sheff Wed | 27 | 10 | 9 | 8 | 36 | 33 | 39 |
| Wimbledon | 26 | 10 | 6 | 10 | 31 | 40 | 36 |
| Norwich | 26 | 9 | 7 | 10 | 25 | 29 | 34 |
| Arsenal | 27 | 8 | 9 | 10 | 30 | 31 | 33 |
| Chelsea | 26 | 8 | 8 | 10 | 34 | 37 | 32 |
| Man City | 26 | 8 | 8 | 10 | 35 | 41 | 32 |
| Aston Villa | 27 | 7 | 10 | 10 | 32 | 36 | 31 |
| Southampton | 26 | 6 | 12 | 8 | 37 | 42 | 30 |
| C Palace | 27 | 7 | 9 | 11 | 31 | 26 | 30 |
| QPR | 25 | 8 | 6 | 11 | 38 | 44 | 30 |
| Everton | 27 | 7 | 9 | 11 | 27 | 36 | 30 |
| West Ham | 26 | 8 | 4 | 14 | 24 | 33 | 28 |
| Coventry | 27 | 6 | 10 | 11 | 25 | 45 | 28 |
| Ipswich | 27 | 5 | 5 | 17 | 29 | 55 | 20 |
| Leicester | 26 | 4 | 6 | 16 | 24 | 45 | 18 |

*Les Ferdinand*
*victorious.*

# February 11

Forest boss Frank Clark warned that some of England's top players are facing a non-stop 12-month work schedule and cannot understand why the PFA is not raising a finger to stop it.

That no-holiday prospect is very much in focus at Forest after defeat at Newcastle reduced the chances of his team qualifying for Europe by conventional means.

If they, and other leading Premiership clubs, do miss the boat then they have one option: to enter the multi-nation Inter Toto Cup, played throughout June and July, with Uefa Cup qualification as the prize.

Clark is dead set against it, points out that players are contractually entitled to four weeks annual holiday but admits he does not have sufficient executive muscle inside his own club to apply a veto.

The Forest manager said: "There are chairmen who think they might draw Inter Milan and people will come and watch that. Whether they will come and watch us play Estonia United I don't know.

"It will ruin the close season and I don't know when players involved in internationals are going to get a holiday. But my chairman is interested, and I am not as powerful as Kevin Keegan.

"I am quite surprised the PFA haven't been more vociferous in their opposition. There's only one organisation which has got the power to do anything about the Premier League or the FA, and that's the PFA."

Only two clubs – Manchester United and Arsenal – have so far lodged direct opposition to the Inter Toto link. Newcastle consider they will be able to bypass it, too, by cruising into Europe under their own steam. If they do, it could, be down to goalkeeper Pavel Srnicek.

Despite his massive popularity among Newcastle fans, Srnicek has suggested his fifth season on Tyneside is to be his last. His contract expires at the end of the season and there has been more talk of a goalkeeping search than discussions about it being renewed.

But his man-of-the-match performance here, which was crucial in seeing Newcastle home, looks as though it has clinched him a new deal.

Keegan confirmed: "Pav has won me over and he will be staying, make no mistake. He has had some very good games for this club but that was the best. We are talking about a contract; we are in discussion."

NEWCASTLE **2**

## NOTTINGHAM FOREST **1**

*(Half-time score : 0-0)*

*Newcastle:* Srnicek, Hottiger, Beresford, Venison, Peacock, Howey, Fox, Lee, Beardsley, Kitson, Gillespie (Bracewell 73).
*Subs:* Watson, Hooper.
*Nottm Forest:* Crossley, Lyttle, Pearce, Cooper, Chettle, Phillips, Gemmill, Collymore, Stone, Woan, Haaland (Lee 73).
*Scorers:* (Newcastle): Fox 47, Lee 73; (Forest): Lee 74.
*Referee:* K Morton (Bury St Edmunds).
*Attendance:* 34,471

| | P | W | D | L | F | A | Pts |
|---|---|---|---|---|---|---|---|
| Blackburn | 28 | 19 | 5 | 4 | 61 | 25 | 62 |
| Man Utd | 28 | 18 | 6 | 4 | 51 | 21 | 60 |
| Newcastle | 28 | 14 | 9 | 5 | 47 | 30 | 51 |
| Liverpool | 27 | 13 | 9 | 5 | 46 | 22 | 48 |
| Nottm Forest | 28 | 13 | 7 | 8 | 41 | 31 | 46 |
| Tottenham | 27 | 12 | 7 | 8 | 45 | 38 | 43 |
| Leeds | 26 | 10 | 9 | 7 | 34 | 28 | 39 |
| Sheff Wed | 29 | 10 | 9 | 10 | 38 | 38 | 39 |
| Aston Villa | 29 | 9 | 10 | 10 | 41 | 38 | 37 |
| Wimbledon | 27 | 10 | 6 | 11 | 32 | 47 | 36 |
| Norwich | 27 | 9 | 8 | 10 | 27 | 31 | 35 |
| Arsenal | 28 | 8 | 10 | 10 | 31 | 32 | 34 |
| Coventry | 29 | 8 | 10 | 11 | 29 | 45 | 34 |
| Chelsea | 27 | 8 | 9 | 10 | 35 | 38 | 33 |
| Man City | 27 | 8 | 8 | 11 | 35 | 44 | 32 |
| Southampton | 27 | 6 | 13 | 8 | 39 | 44 | 31 |
| QPR | 26 | 8 | 7 | 11 | 39 | 45 | 31 |
| Everton | 28 | 7 | 10 | 11 | 29 | 38 | 31 |
| C Palace | 28 | 7 | 9 | 12 | 21 | 28 | 30 |
| West Ham | 28 | 8 | 5 | 15 | 26 | 37 | 29 |
| Ipswich | 27 | 5 | 5 | 17 | 29 | 55 | 20 |
| Leicester | 27 | 4 | 7 | 16 | 25 | 46 | 19 |

Against a side very much prepared to defend and hit out on the break, eternally the Forest way, Newcastle had to work hard for the two-goal lead, furnished by Ruel Fox and Robert Lee but reduced at once by Forest's Jason Lee

But for Srnicek Newcastle would have lost it completely. His late save from Stan Collymore was a stunner. "Even I thought he would score when he started to round me but I knew I at least had to try to stop him," said Srnicek.

*Keith Gillespie is pulled back by Forest defender Alf Inge Haaland.*

# *February 19*

Keith Gillespie put Newcastle into an FA Cup quarter-final for the first time in 19 years and left Andy Dibble reflecting bitterly on a day-time nightmare.

If the young Irish winger will never want to forget the day he grabbed his first two goals for Newcastle, City's anguished keeper definitely will.

Dibble, standing in for the injured Tony Coton, was responsible for the first half of Gillespie's tie-clinching brace in the 18th minute, dropping the clanger of all clangers.

And when, after 64 minutes, this fifth-round tie was finally wrenched away from City, there was a question over whether he and full-back David Brightwell could have done more to stop it happening. Dibble failed to cut out a Peter Beardsley cross and, with Brightwell also caught dawdling, Gillespie steamed in at the far post to finish City and the job off.

That made it an exceptional day for Gillespie, who celebrated his 20th birthday on Saturday and for this performance carried off Sky TV's man-of-the-match award.

Six weeks after moving in as the £1 million make-weight in the Andy Cole deal, it was confirmation of Kevin Keegan's prediction over what a special player he can become.

Gillespie did not sort City out all on his own. Beardsley had too much of a say for that. But when it came to being in the right place at the right time, the former Manchester United speed merchant had no serious rival.

This does not explain what was going through Dibble's mind as he gifted Newcastle the first of their three after 18 minutes. Fifa referee Gerald Ashby provided the controversy to go with the colour that made this such an absorbing afternoon by ignoring a linesman's raised offside flag to give City theoretical advantage as David Brightwell claimed possession.

What happened next is likely to be played over and over again in one of soccer's crazy capers shows. Brightwell, under pressure from Gillespie, passed back to his keeper who had enough time to do half the *Times* crossword before completing his clearance. Instead he put

### NEWCASTLE 3
### MANCHESTER CITY 1
*(Half-time score : 2-1)*

***Newcastle:*** Srnicek, Hottiger, Beresford, Peacock, Howey, Venison, Fox, Lee, Gillespie, Beardsley, Kitson.
***Subs:*** Bracewell, Watson, Hooper.
***Man City:*** Dibble, Summerbee, D. Brightwell (Foster 74), I. Brightwell, Curle, Kernaghan, Gaudino, Flitcroft, Beagrie, Rosler, Quinn (Mike 84).
***Scorers:*** (Newcastle): Beresford 34, Gillespie 18, 64; (City): Rosler 29.
***Referee:*** G Ashby (Worcester).
***Attendance:*** 33,219

one across himself, waited for Gillespie to bear down on him and cracked his clearance against the forward for the ball rebounded over the line.

Keegan said: "I've got Alex Ferguson to thank for not Cup-tying Keith. It would be ironic if we finished up playing Manchester United in the final and he scored the winner."

Yet for a time it seemed that City were set on repeating their Coca-Cola Cup victory on the same ground two months ago. Uwe Rosler, the man Newcastle never seem to handle effectively, equalised after half an hour when Pavel Srnicek produced another goalkeeping howler, dropping Peter Beagrie's corner at the German's feet.

But this tie was clearly meant to fall into Newcastle's hands. How else could a John Beresford cross – admittedly the product of a smart one-two with Beardsley – end up in the top corner of Dibble's net?

That was a fluke goal but a sweet one for Beresford, dumped by City as a kid, and it was his first strike for Newcastle in more than two years.

But the story of the day was Gillespie who gave David Brightwell a chasing and almost had a hat-trick. An angled drive came back off the inside of a post and rolled tantalisingly across the face of Dibble's goal.

However, it was Brightwell and not Dibble whom City boss Brian Horton blamed for the killer goal, the consequences of which heap even more pressure on his shoulders. Horton was convinced Brightwell had time to clear comfortably and said: "You can't wait that long in football. I don't know what he was thinking about."

*Ruel Fox*
*celebrates*
*Gillespie's goal.*

# *February 25*

There comes a time when even footballers of stature do not mind doffing their caps when they know they have been undone by a master. So Dean Saunders doffed his, uncomplainingly, in the direction of two-goal Peter Beardsley.

Beardsley, 34 and clearly not counting, demonstrated for the umpteenth time that class is what he continues to ooze. He did not so much juggle the ball as juggle his feet in the bamboozling preamble to a goal that set the seal on this emphatic Newcastle victory.

When he had completed the routine, defenders Paul McGrath and Gary Charles had the look of men who had tried to negotiate a revolving door clockwise and maybe even blindfolded.

Saunders, who encountered the Beardsley Shuffle when their careers briefly ran in tandem at Liverpool, said: "You know Peter can do that and he's absolutely brilliant at it. But it is his attitude that gets him where he is; he's the same in every game he plays. He is dedicated and wants to do well all of the time.

"Some players get to an age where they think that they've had enough, that they don't need this any more. This one is different. He's got the same level of desire he's always had."

That is why Terry Venables continues to pick Beardsley for England while younger players have long since been discarded and why the Geordie continues to amaze Kevin Keegan, once his playing partner and now his club manager.

Keegan said: "I keep saying to him, 'That's the best goal you've ever scored,' and then he scores an even better one. I get dizzy trying to watch his feet. There's no one living I can think of, or maybe even in the past, who could score a goal like that."

This was a day illuminated by explosive shooting from Newcastle and Villa. Barry Venison might have fancied he had launched a contender for goal of the season when he thumped in the first of the day. Andy Townsend could have submitted his own powerful claim when he clouted in the equaliser from 22 yards. Yet even Beardsley's first goal, which followed a delightful tip-toe through the penalty-area tulips, was a match for those two, never mind his second.

There has always been more to Beardsley's game than finishing,

---

**NEWCASTLE 3**

**ASTON VILLA 1**

*(Half-time score : 1-1)*

*Newcastle:* Srnicek, Hottiger, Beresford, Venison, Peacock, Howey, Lee, Beardsley, Kitson, Fox, Gillespie.
*Subs:* Bracewell, Watson, Hooper.
*Aston Villa:* Bosnich, Charles, Staunton, Teale (Atkinson 84), McGrath, Ehiogu, Yorke, Saunders, Taylor, Johnson, Townsend.
*Scorers:* (Newcastle): Venison 31, Beardsley 55, 66; (Villa): Townsend 40
*Referee:* P Don (Hanworth Park)
*Attendance:* 34,637

though. His innate ability to produce the important and most telling pass is why, ultimately, Villa wilted.

It all made Villa manager Brian Little look over his shoulder in concern as the points gap between the Premiership's most endangered species and his own team shrunk again.

At the end of a bad week Little noted: "The fourth-bottom club are now just eight points behind us, so no one can relax. Any team who hit the wrong spell of form at the wrong time could find themselves down a division."

Newcastle, unbeaten in the League at home for more than a year, have no such worries with Keegan insisting they are still part of a three-horse title race. "I am genuinely still saying that," he said. "We could be the dark horses who do what Leeds did to Manchester United a few years ago."

Keegan's only concern was defender Steve Howey's latest booking which means he will miss the FA Cup quarter-final at Everton.

## League Table After Match

| | P | W | D | L | F | A | Pts |
|---|---|---|---|---|---|---|---|
| Blackburn | 30 | 20 | 6 | 4 | 63 | 26 | 66 |
| Man Utd | 30 | 19 | 6 | 5 | 53 | 22 | 63 |
| Newcastle | 29 | 15 | 9 | 5 | 50 | 31 | 54 |
| Liverpool | 28 | 14 | 9 | 5 | 48 | 23 | 51 |
| Nottm Forest | 30 | 13 | 8 | 9 | 42 | 33 | 47 |
| Leeds | 28 | 11 | 10 | 7 | 35 | 28 | 43 |
| Tottenham | 28 | 12 | 7 | 9 | 46 | 40 | 43 |
| Arsenal | 30 | 10 | 10 | 10 | 35 | 32 | 40 |
| Sheff Wed | 30 | 10 | 9 | 11 | 39 | 40 | 39 |
| Wimbledon | 29 | 11 | 6 | 12 | 35 | 50 | 39 |
| Aston Villa | 31 | 9 | 11 | 11 | 46 | 45 | 38 |
| Coventry | 30 | 9 | 10 | 11 | 33 | 47 | 37 |
| Chelsea | 28 | 9 | 9 | 10 | 37 | 39 | 36 |
| Norwich | 29 | 9 | 9 | 11 | 27 | 33 | 36 |
| Man City | 29 | 9 | 9 | 11 | 37 | 44 | 36 |
| Everton | 30 | 8 | 10 | 12 | 30 | 39 | 34 |
| QPR | 27 | 8 | 8 | 11 | 40 | 46 | 32 |
| Southampton | 28 | 6 | 13 | 9 | 40 | 46 | 31 |
| C Palace | 29 | 7 | 9 | 13 | 21 | 31 | 30 |
| West Ham | 29 | 8 | 5 | 16 | 27 | 39 | 29 |
| Ipswich | 29 | 6 | 5 | 18 | 31 | 58 | 23 |
| Leicester | 29 | 4 | 8 | 17 | 31 | 54 | 20 |

# *February 28*

Kevin Keegan's revitalised side moved within six points of Manchester United and nine of Blackburn after a classy, composed victory at Portman Road.

With only one defeat in 13 games they have moved back within striking distance of the two leaders with 12 games to play. It is certainly no mission impossible, especially if Newcastle can finish the season in the storming style with which they started it.

Keegan said: "I've never given up on the title and we're catching up on the top two now. Yes, I think we can still do it. We would have to go on an incredible run but we could just sneak in by the end of the season. Who's to say what can happen?"

Both goals were from that classical mould: fantastic long-range shots to thrill any crowd. Ruel Fox supplied the first, the perfect response to a night when he was booed for previous East Anglian allegiance to Norwich. Veteran John Wark was booked for a foul on Peter Beardsley and, after a poor clearance from the free-kick, Fox drove an unstoppable shot into the net from 25 yards. It was his 11th goal of the season, making him the club's top scorer.

The second goal, from Paul Kitson, came after 38 minutes and again Wark was at fault, failing to stop a long ball from Darren Peacock. It left Kitson clear and, ignoring Beardsley, he scored with a fierce drive from the edge of the area.

He might have added to his tally, but his best opportunity, in the 70th minute, forced a superb point-blank save from Ipswich keeper Craig Forrest.

What will have pleased Keegan most, even more than victory, was the style of the performance. Newcastle's elegant, one-touch movement has returned, as well as the devastating combination of pace and precision on the counter-attack. "We've learned to win games by grinding them out but we are playing enough good football to keep me happy," Keegan said.

Winger Keith Gillespie, a £1m makeweight in the Andy Cole transfer, is proving a gem. At the heart of it all, though, was the effervescent Beardsley, linking with team-mates and jinking past flat-footed opponents who underlined their status as relegation favourites.

---

## IPSWICH 0

## NEWCASTLE 2
*(Half-time score : 0-2)*

*Ipswich:* Forrest, Yallop, Wark, Linighan, Thompson, Slater (Mason 68), Norfolk, Sedgley, Tanner, Mathie, Chapman.
*Newcastle:* Srnicek, Hottiger, Howey, Peacock, Beresford, Fox, Lee, Venison, Gillespie, Beardsley, Kitson.
*Subs:* Bracewell, Watson, Hooper
*Scorers:* Fox 12, Kitson 38
*Referee:* G Ashby (Worcester)
*Attendance:* 18,639

Striker Alex Mathie, bought from Newcastle by Ipswich last week, fired one shot inches wide and the home side struck the woodwork twice in a minute in a whirlwind first-half spell.

Neil Thompson shot against a post and veteran Lee Chapman saw a bullet header pushed on to the bar. But the gulf in class between top and bottom of the table was always evident.

## *League Table After Match*

|  | P | W | D | L | F | A | Pts |
|---|---|---|---|---|---|---|---|
| Blackburn | 30 | 20 | 6 | 4 | 63 | 26 | 66 |
| Man Utd | 30 | 19 | 6 | 5 | 53 | 22 | 63 |
| Newcastle | 30 | 16 | 9 | 5 | 52 | 31 | 57 |
| Liverpool | 28 | 14 | 9 | 5 | 48 | 23 | 51 |
| Nottm Forest | 30 | 13 | 8 | 9 | 42 | 33 | 47 |
| Leeds | 28 | 11 | 10 | 7 | 35 | 28 | 43 |
| Tottenham | 28 | 12 | 7 | 9 | 46 | 40 | 43 |
| Arsenal | 30 | 10 | 10 | 10 | 35 | 32 | 40 |
| Sheff Wed | 30 | 10 | 9 | 11 | 39 | 40 | 39 |
| Wimbledon | 29 | 11 | 6 | 12 | 35 | 50 | 39 |
| Aston Villa | 31 | 9 | 11 | 11 | 46 | 45 | 38 |
| Coventry | 30 | 9 | 10 | 11 | 33 | 47 | 37 |
| Chelsea | 28 | 9 | 9 | 10 | 37 | 39 | 36 |
| Norwich | 29 | 9 | 9 | 11 | 27 | 33 | 36 |
| Man City | 29 | 9 | 9 | 11 | 37 | 44 | 36 |
| Everton | 30 | 8 | 10 | 12 | 30 | 39 | 34 |
| QPR | 27 | 8 | 8 | 11 | 40 | 46 | 32 |
| Southampton | 28 | 6 | 13 | 9 | 40 | 46 | 31 |
| C Palace | 29 | 7 | 9 | 13 | 21 | 31 | 30 |
| West Ham | 29 | 8 | 5 | 16 | 27 | 39 | 29 |
| Ipswich | 30 | 6 | 5 | 19 | 31` | 60 | 23 |
| Leicester | 29 | 4 | 8 | 17 | 31 | 54 | 20 |

# March 4

Newcastle, with seven wins in their previous eight games, were demolished by Liverpool, prompting Kevin Keegan to depart in fury the stadium where his name will forever be enshrined in legend.

On the day that Andy Cole, the star he transferred for £7 million, helped Manchester United hit nine only the superb goalkeeping of Pavel Srnicek prevented the score reaching Old Trafford proportions.

As Keegan arrived in the Anfield press room a steward announced: "Gentlemen, the manager." And Keegan added "Of the team that didn't turn up."

You could see why he has revised his view that Newcastle remain realistic championship challengers. And with Steve Howey banned and hamstring victim Peter Beardsley doubtful they will need drastic improvement when they return to Merseyside for Sunday's FA Cup quarter-final at Everton.

Beardsley hailed his England and former Kop colleague John Barnes as the mastermind of a Liverpool team he believes can gate-crash the title battle.

Liverpool were so exhilarating that Beardsley, warmly saluted on his latest Anfield return, feels his old club are poised to end their longest sequence without silverware for more than two decades. "This is more like the Liverpool I knew," he declared. "They were top class and they're getting back to their best.

"They got what they deserved against us. From the opening whistle they were first to the ball and I think on the day they were more determined."

Early threats from Keith Gillespie evaporated and after Beardsley's half-time withdrawal Newcastle would have sunk without trace but for Srnicek's heroics. Robbie Fowler's 26th goal of the season and Ian Rush's first league strike for two months broke the Czech's resistance in the second half and stretched Liverpool's run to 23 games with only one defeat.

"We were chasing shadows at times," admitted another Anfield old boy Barry Venison.

The only blot for Liverpool was a booking for Rob Jones that leaves him facing a ban for the clash with Manchester United a fortnight hence.

## LIVERPOOL 2
### NEWCASTLE 0
*(Half-time score : 0-0)*

*Liverpool:* James, Jones, Scales, Ruddock, Babb, McManaman, Barnes, Redknapp, Walters (Thomas 76), Rush, Fowler.
*Newcastle:* Srnicek, Venison, Beresford, Fox (Bracewell 83), Howey, Lee, Beardsley (Watson 45), Hottiger, Peacock, Gillespie, Kitson.
*Sub:* Hooper.
*Scorers:* Fowler 57, Rush 63
*Referee:* P Jones (Loughborough)
*Attendance:* 39,300

At the heart of Liverpool's triumph was the authority of the 'new' Barnes, who is now releasing 21-year-old Jamie Redknapp to find his full potential. "Barnesie ruled the midfield, he kept everything ticking over and he's different class," acclaimed Beardsley.

"He's playing a different role now. But he's such a good player he can play in any position. John is a player, full stop. When you've got the ability he's got he could play left-back. He's that skillful."

The transformation of Barnes from fleet-footed winger to combative midfield fulcrum has been a crucial factor in the remarkable restoration job achieved by Roy Evans. Evans has resurrected the club's pride, power and prestige in little more than a year and he has steered them within sight of their first trophy since the FA Cup three years ago.

"The club is buzzing at the moment. It's a great place to be," said Redknapp, whose shot against the post set up Fowler's opening goal.

That prompted the teenage plunderer to demonstrate a variation of the shirt celebration in front of the old Kop. "I just took my arms out of my sleeves and turned my number round to the front," explained Fowler, who also punished Darren Peacock's woeful back-pass by tee-ing up Rush's goal.

Rush, the 33-year-old skipper, and 31-year-old Barnes were saluted by Evans for spreading the Boot Room gospel amidst the heat of bat-tle. "Having two players like John and Ian is like having a couple of extra coaches on the pitch," revealed Evans.

"They talk to the younger players, like Jamie, and give them the benefit of their great experience. John moans on the field even more than I do off it! "Super passing you expect from him. But his work off the ball and his efforts to get it back when it's lost is what some people did not expect from him. People talk about the need for hard, ball-winning midfielders but Barnesie is no softie. He's got the steel and mental attitude to go out and do the job."

Said Barnes: "I'm getting more and more used to my new role and feeling comfortable with it. I like getting forward. But with so many attackers in the team my job is to sit in front of the back four and I'm happy doing it. As for talking on the field, I've always been a bit of a moaner anyway!"

## League Table After Match

| | P | W | D | L | F | A | Pts |
|---|---|---|---|---|---|---|---|
| Blackburn | 31 | 21 | 6 | 4 | 64 | 26 | 69 |
| Man Utd | 31 | 20 | 6 | 5 | 62 | 22 | 66 |
| Newcastle | 31 | 16 | 9 | 6 | 52 | 33 | 57 |
| Liverpool | 29 | 15 | 9 | 5 | 50 | 23 | 54 |
| Nottm Forest | 31 | 13 | 9 | 9 | 44 | 35 | 48 |
| Tottenham | 29 | 12 | 8 | 9 | 48 | 42 | 44 |
| Leeds | 29 | 11 | 10 | 8 | 35 | 29 | 43 |
| Sheff Wed | 31 | 11 | 9 | 11 | 40 | 40 | 42 |
| Arsenal | 31 | 10 | 10 | 11 | 35 | 33 | 40 |
| Wimbledon | 30 | 11 | 6 | 13 | 36 | 53 | 39 |
| Aston Villa | 32 | 9 | 11 | 12 | 46 | 46 | 38 |
| Coventry | 31 | 9 | 11 | 11 | 33 | 47 | 38 |
| Chelsea | 29 | 9 | 10 | 10 | 37 | 39 | 37 |
| Norwich | 30 | 9 | 10 | 11 | 28 | 34 | 37 |
| Man City | 30 | 9 | 10 | 11 | 38 | 45 | 37 |
| QPR | 28 | 9 | 8 | 11 | 43 | 47 | 35 |
| Everton | 31 | 8 | 11 | 12 | 32 | 41 | 35 |
| Southampton | 29 | 6 | 14 | 9 | 40 | 46 | 32 |
| West Ham | 30 | 9 | 5 | 16 | 28 | 39 | 32 |
| C Palace | 30 | 7 | 10 | 13 | 21 | 31 | 31 |
| Ipswich | 31 | 6 | 5 | 20 | 31 | 69 | 23 |
| Leicester | 30 | 4 | 9 | 17 | 33 | 56 | 21 |

*Robbie Fowler kicks the ball past Pavel Srnicek*
*to score for Liverpool.*

# March 8

## NEWCASTLE 2
### WEST HAM 0
*(Half-time score : 1-0)*

*Newcastle:* Srnicek, Hottiger, Beresford, Howey (Bracewell 84), Peacock, Venison, Fox, Lee, Clark, Gillespie, Kitson (Watson 79).
*Sub:* Hooper
*West Ham:* Miklosko, Breacker, Dicks, Potts, Reiper, Bishop, Hutchison,Hughes, Allen, Rush (Morley 57), Cottee
*Scorers:* Clark 17, Kitson 52
*Referee:* T J Holbrook (Walsall)
*Attendance:* 34,595

Lee Clark bounded back on to the stage he loves to prove that there's life in the young dog yet. Clark, 22, has made only six Premier League starts this season which is why he fears he is going to have to leave Newcastle.

But, asked by Kevin Keegan to fill injured skipper Peter Beardsley's boots, he did so in style. Clark not only came up with Newcastle's opening goal but played an integral part in Paul Kitson's which pushed the hapless Hammers further down the Premiership's slippery relegation slope.

That made it an outstanding night for the midfielder who has just turned down a new contract because he cannot live happily without regular first-team football.

But he looked content enough as Newcastle strolled to a win that adds conviction to their drive to Europe as well as serving as a useful warm-up for Sunday's FA Cup quarter-final tie at Everton.

No doubt that was exactly what Keegan wanted after trudging away from Liverpool with the last shreds of a title challenge blowing in the wind.

It was certainly what Clark wanted as he emphasised after 17 minutes. His first home goal in the Premiership was fashioned from a slick five-man move involving Darren Peacock, Keith Gillespie, Marc Hottiger, Kitson and the scorer. When Kitson brought the move to a climax by whipping his cross low into the six-yard area, Clark came in like a train to rattle the ball in.

"His performance was a vintage one from first to last," said Keegan later. "The goal won't do him any harm and he scored it because of a lot of guts and endeavour. I couldn't have asked more from the whole team. It was everything that Saturday wasn't at Liverpool. They bounced back."

Newcastle had to work harder than they might have imagined to add to Clark's goal. Kitson could have scored sooner had he made better use of a measured pass from Robert Lee. But seven minutes into the second half his tenth goal since joining Newcastle arrived and again the Hammers were flummoxed by a quick bout of inter-passing on the edge of their 18-yard area.

Clark, full of bounce and business-like intent, started it with a pass to Lee, the once-upon-a-time Hammers fan. He provided the perfect opening for Kitson, whose angled shot was simply too good for keeper Ludek Miklosko.

The Hammers did turn up with some attacking intentions because they played with two wingers, Michael Hughes and Matthew Rush. But they were so heavily outplayed that those ambitions were never seriously realised.

They created only one real scoring chance which fell to Rush midway through the second half. But the underworked United keeper Pavel Srnicek was up to it as he charged to the edge of his penalty area to block the winger's effort.

*Clark receives the congratulations of team mates Lee, Venison and Kitson.*

# *March 12*

**EVERTON** 1

**NEWCASTLE** 0

*(Half-time score : 0-0)*

*Everton:* Southall, Jackson, Watson, Unsworth, Ablett, Ebbrell, Horne, Parkinson, Limpar (Stuart 62), Barlow, Ferguson.
*Newcastle:* Srnicek, Hottiger (Watson 80), Venison, Peacock, Beresford (Elliott 50), Lee, Bracewell, Clark, Fox, Kitson, Gillespie.
*Sub:* Hooper.
*Scorer:* L Watson 66
*Referee:* K Cooper (Pontypridd)
*Attendance:* 35,203

Defender Dave Watson showed the strikers the way to goal to secure Everton's passage to a record 23rd FA Cup semi-final. His joyously acclaimed winner for Joe Royle's relegation battlers gives 33-year-old captain Watson the chance to complete the set of domestic honours.

Watson, a pillar of strength at the back for Everton as Newcastle desperately pursued their season's last chance of silverware, made his decisive goal raid in the 66th minute. Graham Stuart, just sent on as substitute for Anders Limpar, was fouled by Marc Hottiger on the left flank. When David Unsworth swung in the free-kick Duncan Ferguson got an almost inevitable flick-on. Hottiger nodded the ball in the air and Watson lunged in for a match-winning header that Pavel Srnicek could only tip despairingly inside his left-hand post. It was Watson's fourth goal of Everton's traumatic season, which could now include a trip to Wembley as Royle's team continue to battle to stay in the Premiership. Watson has already won the League Cup with Norwich and a championship medal with Everton.

Now the remaining domestic prize of an FA Cup winner's medal is within his grasp. But for Watson's counterpart Paul Bracewell, who skippered Newcastle on his return to the ground where he won two championship medals with Everton, it was agony.

The 32-year-old former England midfielder, who has undergone 13 operations and survived a cancer scare, has been a loser in four FA Cup finals. But his hopes of ending that miserable sequence evaporated for another season after a desperately fought but gripping duel.

Everton's meeting with Tottenham will be Everton's first FA Cup semi-final since 1989.

Newcastle, aiming for their first semi-final in the competition since 1974, found their cause severely jolted by the loss of Peter Beardsley, who wrenched a knee in training on Saturday. And early in the second half John Beresford limped out of the action with an ankle injury.

But, even though Unsworth curbed Keith Gillespie's menace, Everton's failure to convert their chances must have given Kevin Keegan and his side hope of at least a St James' Park replay.

Neville Southall, who later made an impressive double save at the near post from Ruel Fox, set up Everton's first glittering scoring opportunity in the 24th minute.

The Wales goalkeeper's long ball was helped on by Ferguson, who will miss the semi-final if referee Paul Durkin refuses to review his decision to dismiss the £4m Scot at Leicester 10 days earlier. From Ferguson's flick Stuart Barlow swept into the box only to see his shot crash against the bar after Srnicek got a hand to it.

On the hour Barlow evaded the pursuing Barry Venison and Darren Peacock after latching on to Gary Ablett's pass. But his shot flew wide of the far post to increase the belief that the tie was heading for a replay. Then came Watson's decisive intervention.

After that Newcastle poured forward. And they came close to equalising in the 79th minute. Hottiger put in Paul Kitson and, when he pulled the ball back, Lee Clark was denied splendidly by Southall and Fox turned the rebound into the side netting.

The victory sends Royle into his second straight semi-final after guiding Oldham there last season when they lost against Manchester United after a replay.

*Watson sees his header go past Srnicek for the winning goal.*

# *March 18*

Peter Beardsley revved up Newcastle's drive for Europe with the sort of goal that leaves even the most inspired goalkeeper demoralised.

Vince Bartram, David Seaman's deputy, had resisted everything that United could throw at him at St James' Park. But in the split second it took for Beardsley's 30-yard drive to speed from foot to net that monument to defiance had been reduced to a pile of rubble.

And the fact that Beardsley, 34, produced it with 25 seconds left on the clock added to the dramatic effect.

Darren Peacock picked out Barry Venison, who spotted Beardsley 25 yards out. The finish was explosive, giving Bartram no chance.

Beardsley missed the FA Cup game at Everton last week because of a knee injury and Newcastle tumbled out. Here he replaced the unlucky Lee Clark but Beardsley's value to the side is immense, as his goal proved.

It also reminded Arsenal's caretaker manager Stewart Houston that, whatever is happening for Arsenal in Europe, the Premiership remains an anxious place for them. Not surprisingly, he was in no mood to salute Beardsley's wonder strike.

Damning it with faint praise, a tetchy Houston said: "It had to be a good strike to beat my goalkeeper the way he played today. But it just goes to show it's not over till the fat lady sings."

Arsenal should hardly have been surprised that Beardsley, sure to be named in Terry Venables' England squad this week, was to be the man to nail them. Since he returned to this, his spiritual home, Beardsley has faced Arsenal four times and scored five goals.

Manager Kevin Keegan had no doubts where this goal stood in the unofficial rankings. "The rest of the lads are waiting for me to say that's the best goal Peter has scored for Newcastle and I'm not going to argue with them," he said. "They aren't making players like him any more."

Arsenal may not generate much sympathy in the hearts of those who watch them but Bartram's tremendous performance definitely did. The £300,000 summer signing from Bournemouth made a string of crucial stops, his first-half save from Robert Lee perhaps the most notable. He also made a splendid save in the opening minutes from Paul Bracewell after Beardsley had set him up.

So inspired was he that it looked as though he would single-handedly grab the point Arsenal wanted, and very much need, for their survival. As usual they played the options, defending solidly as a unit and occasionally breaking from the deep.

Inevitably the closest they came to grabbing a goal involved their Cup Winners' Cup quarter-final hero Ian Wright. Four minutes after half-time he spotted Newcastle keeper Pavel Srnicek off his line and tried to chip him from 25 yards. Srnicek scampered back just in time to push the shot on to the bar and to safety.

Yet Newcastle need not have waited so long to clinch their victory. Paul Kitson had a great chance to catch Bartram out for once but shot straight at the keeper from eight yards, much to the disgust of some among Newcastle's biggest crowd for 10 years.

Keegan remonstrated with fans behind his dug-out appealing for them to back the team, not boo them after the Kitson miss provoked howls of protest. The Newcastle manager did not appear to be greatly impressed with referee Gary Willard either.

Wright looked to have a good claim for a penalty turned down when he was tripped by Robbie Elliott and Newcastle were also bemused by some of the official's decisions.

Keegan said: "I told Stewart Houston at half-time that the penalty rule had been abandoned. But at least he was consistent; he didn't give any."

### League Table After Match

|  | P | W | D | L | F | A | Pts |
|---|---|---|---|---|---|---|---|
| Blackburn | 34 | 23 | 7 | 4 | 70 | 29 | 76 |
| Man Utd | 34 | 21 | 7 | 6 | 63 | 24 | 70 |
| Newcastle | 33 | 18 | 9 | 6 | 55 | 33 | 63 |
| Liverpool | 31 | 16 | 9 | 6 | 54 | 26 | 57 |
| Nottm Forest | 34 | 16 | 9 | 9 | 53 | 38 | 57 |
| Leeds | 32 | 14 | 10 | 8 | 44 | 30 | 52 |
| Tottenham | 32 | 14 | 9 | 9 | 52 | 42 | 51 |
| Wimbledon | 33 | 13 | 6 | 14 | 39 | 54 | 45 |
| Sheff Wed | 35 | 11 | 10 | 14 | 43 | 46 | 43 |
| Coventry | 35 | 10 | 13 | 12 | 37 | 53 | 43 |
| QPR | 31 | 11 | 8 | 12 | 49 | 50 | 41 |
| Man City | 33 | 10 | 11 | 12 | 43 | 50 | 41 |
| Arsenal | 33 | 10 | 10 | 13 | 36 | 37 | 40 |
| Chelsea | 32 | 10 | 10 | 12 | 40 | 45 | 40 |
| Aston Villa | 34 | 9 | 12 | 13 | 46 | 48 | 39 |
| Norwich | 33 | 9 | 12 | 12 | 43 | 38 | 39 |
| Everton | 34 | 9 | 12 | 13 | 37 | 46 | 39 |
| West Ham | 34 | 10 | 7 | 17 | 33 | 44 | 37 |
| C Palace | 32 | 8 | 10 | 14 | 23 | 34 | 34 |
| Southampton | 31 | 6 | 15 | 10 | 41 | 50 | 33 |
| Ipswich | 32 | 6 | 5 | 21 | 31 | 72 | 23 |
| Leicester | 34 | 4 | 9 | 23 | 36 | 66 | 21 |

# *March 22*

---

SOUTHAMPTON **3**

---

NEWCASTLE **1**

*(Half-time score : 0-1)*

*Southampton:* Grobbelaar, Dodd, Benali (Heaney 61), Magilton, Hall, Monkou, Le Tissier, Shipperley, Maddison, Watson, Charlton.
*Newcastle:* Srnicek, Venison, Fox, Howey, Lee, Beardsley, Hottiger, Peacock, Gillespie, Elliott, Kitson.
*Subs:* Bracewell, Watson, Hooper.
*Scorers:* (Southampton): Heaney 86, Watson 89, Shipperley 90; (Newcastle): Kitson 17
*Referee:* J Worrall (Warrington)
*Attendance:* 14,676

Newcastle's faint title hopes were blown away at The Dell as Southampton scored three goals in the last five minutes.

Kevin Keegan's side had been cruising to a regulation victory against the relegation-haunted Saints thanks to a brilliant overhead goal by Paul Kitson.

But in an astonishing finale the home side charged passionately forward and simply overwhelmed Newcastle. All three goals came from inside the six-yard box, down to awful goalkeeping from Pavel Srnicek and non-existent defending.

Substitute Neil Heaney grabbed the first after a goalmouth scramble in the 86th minute when Srnicek failed to hold Jim Magilton's header. In the 89th minute Srnicek was at fault again and this time Gordon Watson, on his home debut, tucked home the loose ball.

Almost immediately the Saints were 3-1 up. Srnicek fumbled a tame shot from Heaney and Neil Shipperley raced in to tap the ball home again. The Czech keeper, so superb for his side this season, must have wondered which particular god he had offended so badly.

Meanwhile the thoughts of Southampton goalkeeper Bruce Grobbelaar at the other end, back playing after conversations with Hampshire police, can only be imagined.

Grobbelaar, in fact, had kept his side in the game for much of the first hour, making a series of excellent stops to deny Newcastle. A flying leap enabled him to tip away a fierce long-range free-kick from Keith Gillespie and he saved with his feet from Kitson and Marc Hottiger. Peter Beardsley, outshining Matt Le Tissier, also went close with a cheeky 40-yard lob that flew just over the bar with Grobbelaar stranded off his line.

In fact, if Le Tissier was trying to prove a point about his England snub, it is no wonder Terry Venables left him out. The Southampton skipper strolled around for most of the first half at walking pace, seemingly oblivious to the intense midfield scrap going on around him.

Newcastle won control thanks to the eager scurrying of the England men Venables did call up: Beardsley, Barry Venison and Robert Lee.

The scorching pace of Gillespie always troubled the home defence and he created a series of chances. Kitson did score in the 18th minute, converting with a brilliant bicycle kick after the home side failed to clear a corner. It should have gone a long way to helping the young striker win over the Newcastle fans still pining for Andy Cole. Instead it was all overshadowed by the most remarkable finish to a match in the Premiership this season.

Southampton manager Alan Ball said: "It has turned us round in an instant. Now we are just behind the pack but with two or three games in hand on our rivals. I was pleased for the players because they never gave up. But I've never experienced a finish like that."

## League Table After Match

| | P | W | D | L | F | A | Pts |
|---|---|---|---|---|---|---|---|
| Blackburn | 34 | 23 | 7 | 4 | 70 | 29 | 76 |
| Man Utd | 35 | 22 | 7 | 6 | 66 | 24 | 73 |
| Newcastle | 34 | 18 | 9 | 7 | 56 | 36 | 63 |
| Nottm Forest | 35 | 17 | 9 | 9 | 56 | 38 | 60 |
| Liverpool | 32 | 16 | 10 | 6 | 54 | 26 | 58 |
| Leeds | 33 | 14 | 10 | 9 | 44 | 33 | 52 |
| Tottenham | 33 | 14 | 10 | 9 | 52 | 42 | 52 |
| Wimbledon | 34 | 14 | 6 | 14 | 41 | 54 | 48 |
| QPR | 32 | 12 | 8 | 12 | 50 | 50 | 44 |
| Sheff Wed | 35 | 11 | 10 | 14 | 43 | 46 | 43 |
| Coventry | 35 | 10 | 13 | 12 | 37 | 53 | 43 |
| Norwich | 34 | 10 | 12 | 12 | 33 | 38 | 42 |
| Man City | 34 | 10 | 11 | 13 | 43 | 52 | 41 |
| Arsenal | 34 | 10 | 10 | 14 | 36 | 40 | 40 |
| Chelsea | 33 | 10 | 10 | 13 | 40 | 46 | 40 |
| Aston Villa | 34 | 9 | 12 | 13 | 46 | 48 | 39 |
| Everton | 34 | 9 | 12 | 13 | 37 | 46 | 39 |
| West Ham | 34 | 10 | 7 | 17 | 33 | 44 | 37 |
| Southampton | 32 | 7 | 15 | 10 | 44 | 51 | 36 |
| C Palace | 32 | 8 | 10 | 14 | 23 | 34 | 34 |
| Ipswich | 33 | 6 | 5 | 22 | 31 | 75 | 23 |
| Leicester | 34 | 4 | 9 | 21 | 36 | 66 | 21 |

# *April 1*

---

CHELSEA **1**

NEWCASTLE **1**

*(Half-time score : 1-0)*

*Chelsea:* Hitchcock, Clarke, Minto, Johnsen, Sinclair (Hopkin 70), Spencer, Furlong, Stein, Peacock,
Spackman, Rocastle (Burley 86).
*Newcastle:* Srnicek, Venison, Bracewell, Fox, Howey, Lee (Clark 78), Beardsley, Hottiger, Peacock, Elliott, Kitson (Watson 66).
*Sub:* Hooper.
*Scorer:* (Chelsea): Peacock ; (Newcastle): Hottiger 88
*Referee:* M J Bodenham (East Looe, Cornwall)
*Attendance:* 22,987

Marc Hottiger salvaged Newcastle a point from a game drifting out of their reach and was then showered with praise for adapting to the Premiership so quickly.

The exciting, attacking Swiss full-back popped up to stab in a close-range rebound seconds from the end. It came as Barry Venison's low drive slipped out of the reach of goalkeeper Kevin Hitchcock, leaving Hottiger with the easiest of chances to score his first goal in the league for Newcastle since his £600,000 move from Switzerland last August.

"Mark is very pacy, has great technical ability and has been performing very well," said England star and team-mate Venison. "Since he has been here he's adjusted to the Premier League very well, to the quick pace and, as he has speed, he is an asset. He will score more goals. That may have been his first but it will not be his last and he has been especially good in the last month."

Hottiger was in the right place at very much the right time to score, giving Keegan's men the point which strengthens their grip on third place. Venison added: "The important thing was that we kept going after they scored. We didn't concede or throw in the towel at any time. We didn't perform well today but still came away with a point.

"Obviously we want to finish as high as we can, which realistically has to be third. We want to fully consolidate our European slot. I'm sure the gaffer is going to build on our squad in the close season but for us this year is far from over yet."

Newcastle saw former St James' Park star Gavin Peacock fire Chelsea ahead before Hottiger earned them a point against a side who now switch their attentions to Europe. Chelsea enter a Cup Winners' Cup duel in Zaragoza carrying the tattered colours of a nation.

"If they progress, we can all stop thinking our game here is rubbish," said Newcastle manager Kevin Keegan of a season scarred by scandal and sleaze. "It would be good for English football, like a shot in the arm. At the start in Europe there was Blackburn, Manchester United and us, and we fancied doing quite well. But we've all fallen, while Chelsea and Arsenal are still there.

"As they say in the wine trade, there's no room for sediments. We must look forward. Chelsea can now go further. They have the best draw and it's not beyond the realms of possibility of them progressing to the final."

Real Zaragoza await Glenn Hoddle's men on Thursday night in the semi-final first leg, some 150 miles from the Bilbao town where Newcastle saw their Uefa Cup dream crushed.

"When we were in Europe I put out our strongest team," added Keegan. "But look at Chelsea. They've had so many injury problems that they even had to call on Graham Rix, with the greatest of respect to him.

"Yet they managed to get through and Glenn now has his injured players back. He can pick the team he wants. I saw them against Bruges, a team of more internationals with greater European experience. But on the night, passion saw Chelsea through.

"People talk about us wanting to be more like the Continentals but you can't ignore the strengths of our game. That was what got Chelsea into Europe in the first place. They've proved to be a very good cup side."

Keegan was off the bench celebrating as his side snatched their late equaliser. But he believes Chelsea have enough to end the season still in the Premiership and celebrating European glory.

"One surprise team will drop out but I don't see it being Chelsea," he said. "These are the places where you want to play."

### League Table After Match

|  | P | W | D | L | F | A | Pts |
|---|---|---|---|---|---|---|---|
| Blackburn | 35 | 24 | 7 | 4 | 72 | 30 | 79 |
| Man Utd | 36 | 22 | 8 | 6 | 66 | 14 | 74 |
| Newcastle | 35 | 18 | 10 | 7 | 57 | 37 | 64 |
| Nottm Forest | 36 | 18 | 9 | 9 | 63 | 39 | 63 |
| Liverpool | 32 | 16 | 10 | 6 | 54 | 26 | 58 |
| Leeds | 34 | 14 | 11 | 9 | 44 | 33 | 53 |
| Tottenham | 34 | 14 | 10 | 10 | 55 | 46 | 52 |
| Wimbledon | 35 | 15 | 6 | 14 | 45 | 57 | 51 |
| QPR | 33 | 13 | 8 | 12 | 51 | 50 | 47 |
| Arsenal | 35 | 11 | 10 | 14 | 41 | 41 | 43 |
| Sheff Wed | 36 | 11 | 10 | 15 | 43 | 53 | 43 |
| Coventry | 36 | 10 | 13 | 13 | 37 | 54 | 43 |
| Aston Villa | 35 | 10 | 12 | 13 | 47 | 48 | 42 |
| Norwich | 35 | 10 | 12 | 13 | 34 | 43 | 42 |
| Chelsea | 34 | 10 | 11 | 13 | 41 | 47 | 41 |
| Man City | 35 | 10 | 11 | 14 | 44 | 54 | 41 |
| Everton | 34 | 9 | 12 | 13 | 37 | 46 | 39 |
| Southampton | 33 | 8 | 15 | 10 | 38 | 48 | 39 |
| C Palace | 33 | 9 | 10 | 14 | 25 | 35 | 37 |
| West Ham | 34 | 10 | 7 | 17 | 33 | 44 | 37 |
| Ipswich | 34 | 6 | 5 | 23 | 31 | 76 | 23 |
| Leicester | 35 | 4 | 9 | 22 | 39 | 79 | 21 |

*Chealsea's Spencer beats Peacock and Hottiger to the ball.*

# *April 8*

NEWCASTLE 3

NORWICH 0

*(Half-time score : 2-0)*

*Newcastle:* Srnicek, Hottiger, Elliott, Venison, Peacock, Howey, Bracewell, Fox, Lee, Beardsley, Kitson.
*Norwich:* Marshall, Prior, Newsome, Polston (Cureton 63), Bradshaw, Crook, Bowen, Milligan, Eadie, Ward, Ullathorne (Sutch 6).
*Subs:* Neilson, Watson, Hooper.
*Scorers:* Beardsley 8 pen. 42, Kitson 74
*Referee:* M Reed (Birmingham)
*Attendance:* 35,518

Europe-bound Newcastle are ready to hand Peter Beardsley a new three-year contract, even though he is nearly 35. And if Kevin Keegan is any judge, it will not be the last Beardsley signs at St James' Park, not by a long chalk.

Newcastle's manager admits his players will laugh when they hear his latest career span prediction for soccer's Peter Pan but he makes it all the same.

The United boss said: "Sir Stanley Matthews played at the top level till he was 50 and Peter could be doing the same at that age if he really wants to.

"That's what he has always said to me: he wants to play forever. He plays every game as though it could be his last but that last game is a long way off. That is what made him the bargain of the century when I brought him back here from Everton for £1.35 million." Even if John Deehan had wanted to, he could not have argued.

Beardsley, who has 12 months of his current deal to run and is on course for a testimonial, was the man who unwittingly tightened still further the rope hanging round Deehan's managerial neck. On his way to helping Newcastle equal a post-war record of 26 home games undefeated.

He scored Newcastle's first goal from the penalty spot after Jon Newsome fouled Paul Kitson and then embarrassed teenage keeper Andy Marshall with a 30-yard bullet for the second, Marshall was kidded into thinking Beardsley was going for a cross. Instead the high-velocity shot whistled in at the near post.

Deehan thinks Norwich will survive but then he would say that. Striker Ashley Ward's gutsy performance apart, there was little in this bland display to suggest they deserve to stay up.

Paul Kitson's 12th Newcastle goal of the season wrapped it all up with the third goal of the day, but that score should have been doubled at least.

Even though Deehan has every reason to fear he is on his way, the Norwich manager's last request was: "If there are going to be any inquests, then let's leave them till the summer. Regardless of who is in charge, who is playing, who is on the board, the most important thing is keeping Norwich in the Premiership.

"Three of our last five games are at home and we've got to make the best of Carrow Road. It will be the ones who show a spirit and stay together who get out of trouble, and we've got spirit in our dressing room."

What they have not got is a Beardsley or anything approaching him in terms of quality. Which is why Keegan wants to sit down and work out a new deal.

He said: "Peter has another year left on his contract but we are going to have to look at that. I don't want anyone pinching him.

"He can't wait for Saturday to come around. He gets in before the staff on match days. I dare say if I asked him to mark out the pitch and put the nets up he would."

### League Table After Match

| | P | W | D | L | F | A | Pts |
|---|---|---|---|---|---|---|---|
| Blackburn............. | 36 | 25 | 7 | 4 | 73 | 30 | 82 |
| Man Utd.............. | 36 | 22 | 8 | 6 | 66 | 24 | 74 |
| Newcastle........... | 36 | 19 | 10 | 7 | 60 | 37 | 67 |
| Nottm Forest.... | 37 | 18 | 10 | 9 | 64 | 40 | 64 |
| Liverpool......... | 34 | 17 | 10 | 7 | 57 | 28 | 61 |
| Leeds................. | 36 | 16 | 11 | 9 | 49 | 33 | 59 |
| Tottenham........... | 34 | 14 | 10 | 10 | 55 | 46 | 52 |
| Wimbledon......... | 35 | 15 | 6 | 14 | 45 | 57 | 51 |
| QPR.................... | 35 | 14 | 8 | 13 | 54 | 52 | 50 |
| Sheff Wed........... | 37 | 12 | 10 | 15 | 45 | 53 | 46 |
| Aston Villa......... | 36 | 10 | 13 | 13 | 47 | 48 | 43 |
| Arsenal.............. | 36 | 11 | 10 | 15 | 42 | 44 | 43 |
| Coventry............ | 36 | 10 | 13 | 13 | 37 | 54 | 43 |
| Norwich.............. | 37 | 10 | 12 | 15 | 34 | 47 | 42 |
| Chelsea.............. | 34 | 10 | 11 | 13 | 41 | 47 | 41 |
| Man City............ | 35 | 10 | 11 | 14 | 44 | 54 | 41 |
| Southampton..... | 34 | 8 | 15 | 11 | 49 | 57 | 39 |
| Everton.............. | 35 | 9 | 12 | 14 | 38 | 48 | 39 |
| C Palace............ | 34 | 9 | 11 | 14 | 25 | 35 | 38 |
| West Ham........... | 35 | 10 | 8 | 17 | 34 | 45 | 38 |
| Leicester............ | 37 | 5 | 9 | 23 | 40 | 71 | 24 |
| Ipswich.............. | 35 | 6 | 5 | 24 | 31 | 80 | 23 |

*Peter Beardsley celebrates his penalty goal.*

# *April 14*

---

EVERTON **2**

NEWCASTLE **0**

*(Half-time score : 1-0)*

*Everton:* Southall, Barrett, Watson, Unsworth, Ablett, Limpar, Horne, Parkinson, Hinchcliffe, Stuart, Amokachi (Grant 63).
*Newcastle:* Hooper, Hottiger (Clark 60), Peacock, Howey, Elliott, Fox (Gillespie 60), Bracewell, Venison, Lee, Beardsley, Kitson.
*Sub:* Harper.
*Scorer:* Amokachi 22, 55
*Referee:* R Gifford(Llanbradach)
*Attendance:* 34,811

Newcastle were taken apart by Daniel Amokachi at Goodison Park as two more goals crowned his six-day transformation from misfit to magician. And Kevin Keegan's team suffered another blow to their chances of a place in Europe when, in the 78th minute, Robert Lee was sent off for a second bookable offence after fouling Andy Hinchcliffe.

Everton's boss Joe Royle could not resist having a swipe at Keegan who had branded the Merseysiders "indisciplined" when Barry Horne and Earl Barrett were sent off at St James' Park earlier in the season. "It was very satisfying to win this game and fitting after the comments that were made by Newcastle about us," he said. "We're not indisciplined. It's ironic that we finished with 11 men tonight. Ironic is a very nice word."

Amokachi, the £3 million Nigerian, has turned his fortunes upside down since he went on as a substitute in Everton's FA Cup semi-final conquest of Tottenham. The two goals he scored at Elland Road that afternoon gave the African a place in Everton folklore but his brace in this match elevated him to a cult status, rivalling Duncan Ferguson who was completing a four-match ban.

Amokachi, given only his third start under Royle because of Paul Rideout's knee injury, scored the first after 22 minutes and guaranteed Everton's victory in the 55th minute.

When the World Cup star, who likes to play from deep rather than as a central striker, limped off in the 63rd minute after a foul by Newcastle's former Goodison favourite Paul Bracewell, he received a standing ovation. Amokachi's goal haul in his last 83 minutes of action has secured Everton's Wembley appearance and gone a long way to keeping them in the Premiership.

His place in attack was one of two changes from the semi-final starting line-up. Royle also recalled Barrett at right-back with Elland Road scorer Matt Jackson dropping to the bench.

The Northern Ireland international Keith Gillespie was a surprise name among the Newcastle substitutes after injury but Keegan kept faith with Bracewell as midfield anchor as Newcastle aimed to avoid a repeat of their FA Cup quarter-final exit at Goodison. Pavel Srnicek's absence with a back injury presented the former Liverpool keeper

Mike Hooper with only his fourth start of the season.

But there was no change in Everton's mood. They exploded into the game and Amokachi gave Hooper a shot to save in the first minute.

Another former Everton star Peter Beardsley, seeking one goal to reach 100 for Newcastle, and join legendary centurions such as Jackie Milburn, Bobby Mitchell and Malcolm Macdonald, soon reminded his old club of his talents. He controlled Lee's 16th-minute cross and brilliantly made space for himself in a crowded box. His left foot shot seemed destined for the net until Neville Southall sprang to his left to save.

Six minutes later the deadlock was broken at the other end and the noise that greeted Amokachi's strike threatened to lift the roof off Goodison. The African forward took three touches to score, controlling the ball from Anders Limpar's long pass, knocking it forward and blasting it right-footed past Hooper.

Amokachi had gone close to scoring before that with a vicious shot off Graham Stuart's header that flew narrowly past Hooper's right hand post. Newcastle's response was a run and cross by Ruel Fox onto the head of Barry Venison. But Southall was perfectly placed to make a comfortable save.

Amokachi doubled Everton's lead 10 minutes after the break with a move he started and finished. Limpar and Hinchcliffe linked on the left. And, when Hooper could only palm up Hinchcliffe's shot, Amokachi swooped to head home.

Keegan said: "I'm not happy and I've spent 25 minutes telling them that. Too many of our players went missing. We lost to a side more committed than we were."

### League Table After Match

|  | P | W | D | L | F | A | Pts |
|---|---|---|---|---|---|---|---|
| Blackburn | 37 | 25 | 8 | 4 | 74 | 31 | 83 |
| Man Utd | 37 | 23 | 8 | 6 | 70 | 24 | 77 |
| Nottm Forest | 38 | 19 | 10 | 9 | 65 | 40 | 67 |
| Newcastle | 37 | 19 | 10 | 8 | 60 | 39 | 67 |
| Liverpool | 36 | 18 | 10 | 8 | 59 | 30 | 64 |
| Leeds | 37 | 16 | 12 | 9 | 50 | 34 | 60 |
| Tottenham | 36 | 15 | 11 | 10 | 58 | 48 | 56 |
| QPR | 37 | 15 | 8 | 14 | 56 | 54 | 53 |
| Wimbledon | 37 | 15 | 7 | 15 | 46 | 61 | 52 |
| Arsenal | 38 | 12 | 10 | 16 | 46 | 46 | 46 |
| Sheff Wed | 38 | 12 | 10 | 16 | 45 | 55 | 46 |
| Coventry | 37 | 11 | 13 | 13 | 39 | 54 | 46 |
| Southampton | 36 | 10 | 15 | 11 | 53 | 58 | 45 |
| Chelsea | 37 | 11 | 12 | 14 | 43 | 50 | 45 |
| Man City | 37 | 11 | 11 | 15 | 47 | 57 | 44 |
| Aston Villa | 37 | 10 | 13 | 14 | 47 | 49 | 43 |
| Everton | 36 | 10 | 12 | 14 | 40 | 48 | 42 |
| Norwich | 38 | 10 | 12 | 16 | 34 | 48 | 42 |
| West Ham | 36 | 11 | 8 | 17 | 37 | 45 | 41 |
| C Palace | 35 | 9 | 12 | 14 | 26 | 36 | 39 |
| Leicester | 38 | 5 | 9 | 24 | 40 | 75 | 24 |
| Ipswich | 37 | 6 | 5 | 26 | 32 | 85 | 23 |

*Daniel Amokachi
in action for
Everton.*

# *April 17*

---

**NEWCASTLE 1**

**LEEDS 2**

*(Half-time score : 1-2)*

*Newcastle:* Srnicek, Hottiger, Elliott (Neilson 50), Watson, Howey, Fox, Lee, Bracewell, Gillespie, Beardsley, Kitson.
*Subs:* Clark, Hooper.
*Leeds:* Lukic, Kelly, Dorigo, Palmer, Wetherall, Pemberton, Speed, McAllister, White (Worthington 73), Yeboah (Masinga 88), Deane.
*Scorers:* (Newcastle): Elliott 30; (Leeds): McAllister 25 pen, Yeboah 31
*Referee:* P Danson (Blaby)
*Attendance:* 35,626

Deadly Tony Yeboah delivered the goal that kept Leeds' Uefa qualification hopes alive and left Kevin Keegan biting his tongue over the refereeing of Paul Danson.

The Newcastle boss stepped back from condemning the way the Leicester official handled this highly charged meeting between two of the Premiership's top six sides. But his actions showed what he thought when he engaged in an animated touchline debate with the official who almost sent off United's Steve Watson in a case of mistaken identity.

Keegan diplomatically claimed later: "We didn't discuss anything but I thought we were going to see what would have been a ridiculous sending-off. I can't answer for the referee. Why should I?"

Danson, who mistakenly sent off West Ham's Alvin Martin earlier in the season, almost did it again, showing Watson a red card because he thought he had booked him once and was ready to hand out a second censure. Only when players pointed out the error did Danson reach for the yellow card.

That chaotic sideshow did not deflect Leeds from their mission of becoming the first Premiership side in 15 months to win a league game at St James' Park.

They scored the first from a penalty after Watson had inexplicably palmed away Tony Dorigo's cross to give Gary McAllister his fifth goal of the season. And, although Newcastle equalised through Robbie Elliott within five minutes, it took Leeds little more than 60 seconds to reclaim the lead.

Again it was a piece of naive defending that cost Newcastle dearly. The whole back four was caught out as Gary Speed played Yeboah through with a pass from deep. To compound collective error, Pavel Srnicek came charging out and was easily sidestepped by Yeboah who, in almost mocking style, rolled in his 11th goal in 13 games.

Paul Kitson missed Newcastle's best chance for an equaliser, shooting at John Lukic from five yards.

Although Leeds boss Howard Wilkinson insisted of fifth-placed Newcastle, "I'd rather be where they are they are, in the driving seat," Keegan acknowledged Leeds' right to a win that complicates

Newcastle's once automatic looking route into Europe.

Elliott's season is over and he faces the prospect of his third cruciate knee ligament operation. Winger Keith Gillespie was also in the wars and went to hospital afterwards with facial injuries.

*Carlton Palmer of Leeds.*

# *April 29*

---

**MANCHESTER CITY 0**

**NEWCASTLE 0**

*(Half-time score : 0-0)*

*Manchester City:* Coton (Burridge 45), Phelan, Curle, Walsh (Beagrie 62), Quinn, Flitcroft, Kernaghan, Summerbee, Simpson (Gaudino 54), Edghill, Rosler.
*Newcastle:* Srnicek, Beresford, Bracewell, Fox, Howey, Beardsley, Clark, Hottiger, Peacock, Gillespie, Watson.
*Subs:* Neilson, Allen, Hooper.
*Referee:* G Poll (Tilehurst)
*Attendance:* 27,389

John Burridge felt like a character plucked from the silver screen as he launched the sort of comeback that happens only on the last page of a Hollywood script. And the 43-year old Manchester City goalkeeper, who continues to defy standard football retirement law, had no problem deciding which one he had to be.

"When I ran out there, I felt just like Forrest Gump," said a deadly serious Burridge."Newcastle fans were cheering me on, City fans were willing me to do well. I was so emotional, I felt like crying."

Laugh if you will. Budgie will not care. He knows that at least one half of football has been laughing for years at the antics he prefers to define as pure dedication.

Whichever version is preferred, one indisputable fact remains about English football's answer to the Gump-style all-American hero: years after younger rivals have called it a day, he is still around – and around in the Premiership at that.

His six year exile from such territory ended when an injury to City keeper Tony Coton obliged him play the entire second half at Maine Road. And while Newcastle, who employ him as a part-time goalkeeping coach, hardly put him to much of a test Burridge nevertheless produced a clean sheet, the equivalent, he has always believed, of a striker's hat-trick.

That left him to reaffirm: "There's no retirement date in my mind. Why should I stop? At this rate I could still be playing at 50. But that's goalkeeping; at this level you need somebody who has done what I call National Service, two or three years down in the lower leagues.

"When I was young, I couldn't wait for the game to end. It was purgatory for me, I was so damn nervous. But over the past five years I have learned how to eat, how to relax and I don't make mistakes, which is what goalkeepers are judged on."

Burridge's relaxation theory is not in the mind. He has taught himself self-hypnosis techniques and, while Coton laboured on till half-time, the veteran slipped back to the dressing-room to warm up his mind. "I don't like to call it being in a trance; it's more focusing on what I am about to do and relaxing," explained a man who last played in the top flight for Southampton at Spurs in 1989.

Such was the low quality nature of this match that fans could just as easily have dropped off too. Newcastle were without too many of their better players to be confident about stepping up their faltering bid for Europe. City just seemed grateful to pick up a survival point.

That is why the Burridge sideshow became the big picture and, as the credits rolled, he headed home to watch *Match of the Day* with wife Janet who knew he'd be sitting in front of the telly wearing his goal-keeping gloves. He always does. By his side there was a football ready to take to bed.

"There's nothing wrong with that," he said, "I like the smell of the leather. There's a lot more wrong with drinking alcohol till two or three in the morning. Normally there's no fat in my diet but on Saturday nights I do like to give myself a treat. I like a chocolate digestive and a packet of cheese-and-onion crisps."

## League Table After Match

|              | P  | W  | D  | L  | F  | A  | Pts |
|--------------|----|----|----|----|----|----|-----|
| Blackburn    | 40 | 26 | 8  | 6  | 78 | 37 | 86  |
| Man Utd      | 38 | 23 | 9  | 6  | 70 | 24 | 78  |
| Nottm Forest | 40 | 21 | 10 | 9  | 69 | 41 | 73  |
| Liverpool    | 38 | 20 | 10 | 8  | 63 | 31 | 70  |
| Newcastle    | 39 | 19 | 11 | 9  | 61 | 41 | 68  |
| Leeds        | 39 | 18 | 12 | 9  | 53 | 35 | 66  |
| Tottenham    | 38 | 16 | 12 | 10 | 60 | 49 | 60  |
| QPR          | 39 | 15 | 8  | 16 | 56 | 56 | 53  |
| Wimbledon    | 39 | 15 | 8  | 16 | 46 | 63 | 53  |
| Arsenal      | 40 | 13 | 11 | 16 | 51 | 47 | 50  |
| Southampton  | 38 | 11 | 16 | 11 | 55 | 58 | 49  |
| Chelsea      | 39 | 12 | 13 | 14 | 44 | 50 | 49  |
| Man City     | 39 | 12 | 12 | 15 | 50 | 59 | 48  |
| Sheff Wed    | 40 | 12 | 12 | 16 | 45 | 55 | 48  |
| Coventry     | 38 | 11 | 13 | 14 | 39 | 56 | 46  |
| West Ham     | 38 | 12 | 9  | 17 | 40 | 46 | 45  |
| Everton      | 38 | 10 | 14 | 14 | 40 | 48 | 44  |
| Aston Villa  | 39 | 10 | 13 | 16 | 47 | 54 | 43  |
| C Palace     | 38 | 10 | 12 | 16 | 29 | 40 | 42  |
| Norwich      | 40 | 10 | 12 | 18 | 35 | 51 | 42  |
| Leicester    | 40 | 6  | 9  | 25 | 42 | 77 | 27  |
| Ipswich      | 39 | 6  | 6  | 27 | 33 | 88 | 24  |

# *May 3*

---

### NEWCASTLE 3
### TOTTENHAM 3
*(Half-time score : 2-3)*

*Newcastle:* Srnicek, Hottiger, Beresford, Peacock, Howey, Bracewell (Allen 45), Fox (Hooper 55), Gillespie, Watson, Beardsley, Lee.
*Sub:* Clark.
*Tottenham:* Walker, Austin, Edinburgh, Calderwood, Mabbutt, Barmby (Campbell 67), Howells, Anderton, Rosenthal, Sheringham, Klinsmann.
*Scorers:* (Newcastle): Gillespie 7, Peacock 10, Beardsley 70; (Tottenham): Barmby 22, Klinsmann 24, Anderton 26
*Referee:* D Gallagher (Banbury)
*Attendance:* 35,603

Jurgen Klinsmann's missed penalty had probably cost Spurs a place in Europe and White Hart Lane the prospect of watching the Footballer of the Year in action next season. No wonder manager Gerry Francis joked to the Newcastle tea lady, "How about a bit of heroin?"

Klinsmann, the man who can do no wrong in North London, had the chance to amplify that point at St James' Park. Spurs were 3-2 up and won themselves a 55th-minute penalty in controversial circumstances. But instead of putting it away the German superstar struck his shot against the legs of Newcastle's substitute keeper Mike Hooper.

The irony of that match-turning moment was that Hooper had only just arrived on the pitch following the sending-off of Pavel Srnicek for bringing down Nicky Barmby. Referee Dermot Gallagher, who later sent off Colin Calderwood for a second bookable offence, showed Srnicek the red card, infuriating United fans and even some Spurs players.

It looked for all the world as though he had made a genuine attempt to win the ball but Gallagher turned a deaf ear even when Spurs striker Teddy Sheringham lodged a protest.

Newcastle began impressively, going two up in 10 minutes as first Keith Gillespie and then Darren Peacock grabbed their first league goals for Newcastle, both headers.

Klinsmann led a Spurs comeback that brought them three goals in four amazing minutes. First he exchanged passes with Barmby before the young midfielder drove in the first Spurs goal. Then Klinsmann grabbed his 29th goal of the season, ghosting in at the far post to turn the match around. If that was hot stuff, Darren Anderton's 22-yarder was a stormer as he made it 3-2. Srnicek, a keeper on the top of his form, did not to move a muscle before Anderton's drive had hit the top corner.

Just when it looked as though Spurs were going to take the vital points they need for Europe they were undone as Peter Beardsley grabbed his 15th goal of the season after 70 minutes. The Newcastle skipper powered through Spurs' defence and drove beyond Ian Walker.

Though the result was a disappointment for Geordie fans, whose own European hopes are in jeopardy, they still gave both teams a standing ovation at the end. It was pure entertainment from start to finish with referee Gallagher the only man on the pitch failing to win himself a cheer.

But the reality of the consequences quickly dawned on Spurs players once they were back in the dressing-room. As Francis explained: "Coming to Newcastle and getting a 3-3 draw would normally be considered a good result especially as they've only lost here once in the league this season.

"But the heads are down in the dressing-room because they know what an important game this was. However, if I had said back in November that this club would reach the semi-finals of the FA Cup and be pushing for a place in Europe, I think I would have been accused of having been out on the local brew."

Newcastle manager Kevin Keegan said: "That's the greatest advertisement I have seen for football this season. Football was the winner and I am pleased about that even though the result doesn't help either club."

## *League Table After Match*

|  | P | W | D | L | F | A | Pts |
|---|---|---|---|---|---|---|---|
| Blackburn | 40 | 26 | 8 | 6 | 78 | 37 | 86 |
| Man Utd | 40 | 25 | 9 | 6 | 74 | 26 | 84 |
| Nottm Forest | 41 | 22 | 10 | 9 | 70 | 41 | 76 |
| Liverpool | 40 | 20 | 11 | 9 | 63 | 33 | 71 |
| Newcastle | 40 | 19 | 12 | 9 | 64 | 44 | 69 |
| Leeds | 40 | 19 | 12 | 9 | 55 | 36 | 69 |
| Tottenham | 40 | 16 | 13 | 11 | 64 | 54 | 61 |
| QPR | 41 | 16 | 9 | 16 | 58 | 57 | 57 |
| Wimbledon | 41 | 15 | 10 | 16 | 46 | 63 | 55 |
| Southampton | 40 | 12 | 17 | 11 | 58 | 59 | 53 |
| Arsenal | 41 | 13 | 12 | 16 | 51 | 47 | 51 |
| Chelsea | 41 | 12 | 15 | 14 | 48 | 54 | 51 |
| Man City | 41 | 12 | 13 | 16 | 51 | 61 | 49 |
| Sheff Wed | 41 | 12 | 12 | 17 | 45 | 56 | 48 |
| Aston Villa | 41 | 11 | 14 | 16 | 50 | 55 | 47 |
| West Ham | 40 | 12 | 10 | 18 | 40 | 47 | 46 |
| Everton | 40 | 10 | 16 | 14 | 43 | 51 | 46 |
| Coventry | 40 | 11 | 13 | 16 | 41 | 61 | 46 |
| C Palace | 40 | 11 | 12 | 17 | 31 | 43 | 45 |
| Norwich | 41 | 10 | 12 | 19 | 36 | 53 | 42 |
| Leicester | 41 | 6 | 10 | 25 | 43 | 78 | 28 |
| Ipswich | 40 | 7 | 6 | 27 | 35 | 88 | 27 |

# *May 8*

---

**BLACKBURN 1**

NEWCASTLE 0

*(Half-time score : 1-0)*

---

*Blackburn:* Flowers, Kenna,
Sherwood, Hendry, Le Saux,
Ripley (Slater 81), Shearer,
Sutton, Berg, Batty, Pearce.
*Newcastle:* Srnicek, Beresford,
Fox, Howey, Lee, Beardsley,
Clark, Hottiger, Peacock,
Gillespie, Watson.
*Subs:* Neilson, Allen, Hooper.
*Scorer:* Shearer 29
*Referee:* P Don (Middlesex)
*Attendance:* 30,545

---

The head of Alan Shearer, the hands of Tim Flowers and the hearts of an adoring public made it a special VE Day evening for Blackburn as their first title success for 81 years came into sharp and colourful focus.

Victory at Ewood was the event most of the 30,545 fans were celebrating on a chill night in East Lancashire but not before the sirens had sounded and referee Phil Don had generously ignored a blatant Newcastle penalty.

On a day when stirring film of the war years had flickered across the TV screens this night might aptly have been renamed by Blackburn fans The Great Escape.

It will not matter to them, of course, that for much of this game Flowers was conducting a personal crusade to keep Alan Shearer's 29th minute lead intact. They will overlook Colin Hendry's trip on Keith Gillespie two minutes from time inside the penalty area, for over a long season these breaks tend to even themselves out. Did not Manchester United get a lucky break here?

Newcastle discovered form that has eluded them for all but one of the last 16 away games to make it an agonising night for Blackburn. Their benefactor Jack Walker had kicked off the evening by promising from the centre-circle he would do all in his power to keep Shearer at Blackburn, just in case the Geordie hordes from among whom Shearer originated thought otherwise.

Newcastle, having beaten Blackburn three times this season, were up for the game once they had survived the ferocity of Blackburn's opening assault. Had Chris Sutton – two goals in his last 23 games – been in more confident form he might have made more of an early chance.

When the goal came it was the indirect result of a poor back-header from Steve Watson, which had Pavel Srnicek off his line to intercept, the ball ping-ponging about to Sutton then David Batty. Their shots were blocked and the ball spun to Graeme Le Saux, whose chip to the far post was met by Shearer, leaning on Marc Hottiger to get purchase on the header.

This did nothing more than stir Newcastle into action, with Peter

Beardsley probing for space in the Blackburn defence. He seemed to have found it as the nimble-footed Ruel Fox rolled the ball to him a minute from halftime. How Flowers tipped the shot over could best be explained by a PE instructor. That, as it turned out, was just his warm up for, as the second half unfolded, Flowers' acrobatics became more spectacular.

He made a stunning, low, one-handed save to a sharp shot from Fox, propelled himself to a searing shot from Robert Lee that was heading for the top corner and made a backbreaking dive to deny John Beresford.

Meanwhile Blackburn threatened only on the occasional break, although Shearer showed fans who believe otherwise that he is human when he screwed one shot across the face of goal and drove another at Srnicek's legs.

"That was bottle that you saw out there tonight," said Flowers later. "We are going to fight to the death. We will go out and give 100 per cent just like we have all season."

Blackburn manager Kenny Dalglish said: "That was my best ever night at the club. The lads really stood up to be counted tonight. They responded magnificently and it was a marvellous occasion for the people of Blackburn. I'm sure Jack Walker was excited and he should certainly be proud."

Gillespie, surprisingly, backed referee Don's decision not to award a penalty. "I know in my own mind that it was the right decision," he said.

Newcastle boss Kevin Keegan, who saw his side's hopes of a Uefa Cup place slip further away, added: "From the bench it looked a certain penalty. But, if the lad said it wasn't, then that must be right. I think we deserve a place in Europe on the season's performances but you don't always get what you deserve as we saw tonight and it is in other people's hands now. Their keeper pulled off some world-class saves and I just don't know how we didn't score."

### League Table After Match

| | P | W | D | L | F | A | Pts |
|---|---|---|---|---|---|---|---|
| Blackburn | 41 | 27 | 8 | 6 | 79 | 37 | 89 |
| Man Utd | 40 | 25 | 9 | 6 | 74 | 26 | 84 |
| Nottm Forest | 41 | 22 | 10 | 9 | 70 | 41 | 76 |
| Liverpool | 40 | 20 | 11 | 9 | 63 | 33 | 71 |
| Newcastle | 41 | 19 | 12 | 10 | 64 | 45 | 69 |
| Leeds | 40 | 19 | 12 | 9 | 55 | 36 | 69 |
| Tottenham | 40 | 16 | 13 | 11 | 64 | 54 | 61 |
| QPR | 41 | 16 | 9 | 16 | 58 | 57 | 57 |
| Wimbledon | 41 | 15 | 10 | 16 | 46 | 63 | 55 |
| Southampton | 40 | 12 | 17 | 11 | 58 | 59 | 53 |
| Arsenal | 41 | 13 | 12 | 16 | 51 | 47 | 51 |
| Chelsea | 41 | 12 | 15 | 14 | 48 | 54 | 51 |
| Man City | 41 | 12 | 13 | 16 | 51 | 61 | 49 |
| Sheff Wed | 40 | 12 | 12 | 16 | 45 | 55 | 48 |
| Aston Villa | 41 | 11 | 14 | 16 | 50 | 55 | 47 |
| West Ham | 40 | 12 | 10 | 18 | 40 | 47 | 46 |
| Everton | 40 | 10 | 16 | 14 | 43 | 51 | 46 |
| Coventry | 40 | 11 | 13 | 16 | 41 | 61 | 46 |
| C Palace | 40 | 11 | 12 | 17 | 31 | 43 | 45 |
| Norwich | 41 | 10 | 12 | 19 | 36 | 53 | 42 |
| Leicester | 41 | 6 | 10 | 25 | 43 | 78 | 28 |
| Ipswich | 40 | 7 | 6 | 27 | 35 | 88 | 27 |

# *May 14*

---

NEWCASTLE 3

---

CRYSTAL PALACE 2

*(Half-time score : 3-0)*

*Newcastle:* Srnicek, Hottiger, Beresford, Howey, Peacock, Watson, Fox, Gillespie, Clark, Lee, Beardsley.
*Subs:* Neilson, Allen, Hooper.
*Palace:* Martyn, Gordon, Pitcher, Young, Shaw, Southgate, Houghton, Newman (Cox 81), Salako (Dyer 45), Armstrong, Dowie.
*Scorers:* (Newcastle): Fox 6, Lee 26, Gillespie 28; (Palace): Armstrong 51, Houghton 81.
*Referee:* G Ashby (Worcester).
*Attendance:* 35,626

Ruel Fox gave Palace the push all the way down into the First Division.

What was meant to be a fight to the bitter end didn't exactly work out that way for a side whose last stand effectively lasted six minutes.

That was how long Fox took to produce the first of three first half goals that put the lights out on Alan Smith's career as a Premiership boss.

Yet if Smith knows with stone cold certainty where his bleak future lies, Newcastle and their UEFA Cup qualification hopes are still up in the air.

With Leeds avoiding defeat at Spurs, Newcastle now have to hope that Manchester United recover from championship trauma to win the FA Cup, thereby releasing an extra European place.

That situation sums up the very nature of their season, and it was all encapsulated in the final 90 minutes of the 94 - 95 campaign.

They set off, just as they did in August, on a high, looking as though they were going to wipe the floor with Palace having struck out in front after six minutes.

Fox gave them that flyer firing in from 20 yards off the boot of Ray Houghton.

Then they blitzed Smith's sorry side with two goals in two minutes with Fox conjuring up further difficulties for the Premiership's one-season wonders.

He showed good wing skills to get to the line and plant a cross on to Robert Lee's head for the England midfielder to claim his 15th goal of the season.

Before Palace had time to get their wind back they were hit by another, Keith Gillespie curling a 20 yarder beyond Nigel Martyn.

But instead of nailing Palace to the floor, Newcastle allowed them off the deck where they reclaimed some end of season dignity.

Six minutes after half time, Chris Armstrong, who remains a Newcastle target, stole in at the near post to head in Gareth Southgate's cross.

That was bad enough for Newcastle but worse was to follow, and eight minutes from time, Houghton took a pass from substitute Bruce

Dwyer to slot past Pavel Srnicek.

But neither that goal nor any of the four which preceded it formed the abiding memory.

What did was the sight of Smith turning on his heel just before disappearing down the tunnel – and offering Palace fans one last farewell wave.

|              | P  | W  | D  | L  | F  | A  | Pts |
|--------------|----|----|----|----|----|----|-----|
| Blackburn    | 42 | 27 | 8  | 7  | 80 | 39 | 89  |
| Man Utd      | 42 | 26 | 10 | 6  | 77 | 28 | 88  |
| Nottm Forest | 42 | 22 | 11 | 9  | 72 | 43 | 77  |
| Liverpool    | 42 | 21 | 11 | 10 | 65 | 37 | 74  |
| Leeds        | 42 | 20 | 13 | 9  | 59 | 38 | 73  |
| Newcastle    | 42 | 20 | 12 | 10 | 67 | 47 | 72  |
| Tottenham    | 42 | 16 | 14 | 12 | 66 | 58 | 62  |
| QPR          | 42 | 17 | 9  | 16 | 61 | 59 | 60  |
| Wimbledon    | 42 | 15 | 11 | 16 | 48 | 65 | 56  |
| Southampton  | 42 | 12 | 18 | 12 | 61 | 63 | 54  |
| Chelsea      | 42 | 13 | 15 | 14 | 50 | 55 | 54  |
| Arsenal      | 42 | 13 | 12 | 17 | 52 | 49 | 51  |
| Sheff Wed    | 42 | 13 | 12 | 17 | 49 | 57 | 51  |
| West Ham     | 42 | 13 | 11 | 18 | 44 | 48 | 50  |
| Everton      | 42 | 11 | 17 | 14 | 44 | 51 | 50  |
| Coventry     | 42 | 12 | 14 | 16 | 44 | 62 | 50  |
| Man City     | 42 | 12 | 13 | 17 | 53 | 64 | 49  |
| Aston Villa  | 42 | 11 | 15 | 16 | 51 | 56 | 48  |
| C Palace     | 42 | 11 | 12 | 19 | 34 | 49 | 45  |
| Norwich      | 42 | 10 | 13 | 19 | 37 | 54 | 43  |
| Leicester    | 42 | 6  | 11 | 25 | 45 | 80 | 29  |
| Ipswich      | 42 | 7  | 6  | 29 | 36 | 93 | 27  |

*Ruel Fox celebrates after scoring against Palace.*

# The
# Players

## Pavel Srnicek

Pavel Srnicek stands over six feet tall and higher still in the estimation of Newcastle fans. The one-time Czech soldier is firmly entrenched as the club's No 1 goalkeeper, even if getting there has been quite a battle. When Jim Smith signed him from Banik Ostrava for £350,000 in the winter of 1991, Srnicek could not speak a word of English. He admits the language barrier stood in the way of any real football progress at St James' Park even though he had played in the Uefa Cup for Ostrava against Aston Villa. It did not help his cause either that within weeks of his arrival on Tyneside, Smith was sacked and replaced by Ossie Ardiles.

Initially Srnicek was handicapped by the image that he was a 'typical' Continental, punching crosses he should have caught, missing crosses he could have punched. So it was little wonder that in his early days he had to play second fiddle, first to the ageless John Burridge, then the Irishman Tommy Wright, now of Nottingham Forest.

What has never been in doubt is Srnicek's outstanding ability as a shot-stopper. He is superbly athletic. That quality was very much in evidence during the 1994-95 season in which he has convinced Kevin Keegan, initially a doubter, that he ranks among the best four keepers in the Premiership.

If Pav, who recently signed a new three-year contract, wanted to give anyone credit for that, the honour would probably be his six year-old daughter Vendy. Vendy was only two when the Srniceks landed on Tyneside but once she started school dad benefited. The youngster came from her classroom lesson and helped Pav improve his English beyond recognition.

He is now now not just a fluent English speaker but also a cult figure at Newcastle, so that Mike Hooper, brought in by Keegan from Liverpool to replace him, languishes in the reserves.

In the eyes of United fans one moment in an impressive season stands out as far as Srnicek is concerned. That was the save he made against Forest's Stan Collymore back in February at St James'. It earned United three points and Srnicek a standing ovation.

# Marc Hottiger

Marc Hottiger is as reliable as a Swiss clock but then the quiet man of St James' originates from Lausanne.

That is not where Kevin Keegan found him last summer. The manager went to the World Cup in America to secure his £520,000 bargain. Keegan rated him the best attacking defender in the tournament and other managers must have thought so too.

Newcastle had to beat off competition from Everton and Borussia Moenchengladbach to sign him from the Swiss club FC Sion. In the beginning, it looked as though Hottiger, 27, would face strong competition for a Premiership place. He did lose his full-back berth for a four-game spell early in the season to Steve Watson but he came back strongly to make the position his own.

In playing style he is not dissimilar to Gary Kelly of Leeds, who loves to get forward and as a consequence risks accusations of being unable to defend.

The attacking instinct is firmly traceable. When he launched his football career back home as a part-timer with Second Division club Renens he was an out-and-out winger. He switched when he moved into the First Division with Lausanne Sports in 1988.

Despite the early hiccup Hottiger has handled the transition from Swiss to English football amazingly well. At least that is the view of his international team boss Roy Hodgson, the Englishman who took Switzerland to the World Cup finals for the first time in 30 years and now targets the European Championships.

"What I admire about him is the way he came straight out of a tiring, demanding competition like the World Cup and straight into a country where he didn't speak a word of the language, totally on his own," says Hodgson. "It is very much to his credit that he not only survived but, as far as I can see, came through with flying colours." At least Hottiger, on course for his 50th cap, did not go through his first season in England waiting to register his first goal, as many defenders do. He secured that back in January at Ewood Park where Newcastle pulled off a shock FA Cup replay win. He was also on the mark against Chelsea, on April 1, when he scored Newcastle's equaliser in a 1-1 draw.

# Steve Howey

Steve Howey's season started as something of a trial and before long was transformed into something of a treat.

The 1994-95 campaign was supposed to be about trying to establish whether he could make it as a Premier League defender. Howey delivered the answer so emphatically that within months Terry Venables handed him his England debut against Nigeria.

That sums up the astonishing emergence in top-flight soccer of the Sunderland-born player who began his Newcastle career as a striker and looked as though he was heading nowhere fast. This is his senior games-and-goals record over his first three seasons: 1988-89, P 1 Gls 0; 1989-90, P 0 G 0; 1990-91, P 11 G 0. But from the day Keegan walked into St. James' he saw something else in the player his United mates call "The Boy". Keegan reckoned he was not a centre-forward at all but a central defender in the Alan Hansen mould.

That judgment was largely substantiated as Howey helped Newcastle to promotion from the old Second Division but he had still to prove himself against the best.

It did not help that in his first year in the Premiership, he was plagued by groin trouble and underwent four operations. That meant he played only 13 games. This time around has been injury-free and he has simply got better and better. Yet when he heard his England call up on his car-phone, Howey still thought it was a Keegan wind-up.

It was only when Keegan's secretary delivered air travel information needed for the link-up with England that Howey, whose brother Lee is a striker on Sunderland's books, accepted it was true. He played alongside Liverpool's Neil Ruddock against the Nigerians as England won 1-0 thanks to David Platt's goal.

Howey has two odd memories of the night. One was trying to shoulder-charge Everton's Daniel Amokachi and feeling as though he had bounced off a rock. The other was the after-match celebratory meal: a sandwich and a packet of crisps at an M1 service station as he headed back to Tyneside. He was in the big-time.

Howey's quick and cultured style should ensure that he stays there.

# Philippe Albert

Philippe Albert's season came to a shuddering halt as he was about to ring in the New Year after celebrating his first Geordie Christmas.

The big bouncing Belgian was taking part in a five-a-side match at United's Maiden Castle training ground as he prepared for what should have been his 18th Premiership appearance of the season at Norwich. Suddenly, and for no apparent reason; "Prince" Albert crumpled in a heap. An early examination, conducted by physio Derek Wright, raised fears that he had damaged cruciate knee ligaments. Albert was whisked off to a top specialist. Wright's initial diagnosis proved spot-on.

There are those who would argue that, in that moment, Newcastle's championship ambitions also collapsed. At the time, they were lying third and there was every reason to suppose they would mount a much more serious challenge than they actually mustered.

One thing is certain: from the moment the man from the Ardennes region of Belgium bowed out and began the long road back, United were never quite the same side.

Albert had announced his arrival with an impressive performance on the opening Sunday of the season when Newcastle went to newly promoted Leicester and registered a 3-1 win.

Albert, given the No 27 shirt because he was signed by Kevin Keegan on his 27th birthday, did not score at Filbert Street, yet did everything but, including picking up his first booking in English football. Keegan and Magpie fans were more than happy with what they saw from a man who had proved he was the outstanding player he looked, playing and scoring for Belgium in the World Cup. Keegan had wanted to sign him from Anderlecht for more than a year and feared he would lose him to one of the big Italian clubs. But Newcastle got their man for £2.7 million.

Albert, the son of a factory worker, showed himself to be a cavaliering attacker as well as one of the Premier League's best central defenders. He scored his first goal in England in the Coca-Cola Cup in October. When Leicester played the return fixture at St. James' Park on December 10, he went one better, scoring twice in a 3-1 win.

# John Beresford

John Beresford has been in the England squad but did not quite fulfill his big ambition to win a first full cap. Team-mates say, never mind playing for his country, Bez could talk for England.

Keegan, though, is sure the Sheffield-born full-back has plenty of other attributes. That is why he paid Portsmouth £650,000 in June 1992 – one of his first signings.

Beresford, an attacking full-back, was so sure it was a big move that he turned down the chance to join Sheffield Wednesday, then firmly established as a Premier League club. The transfer worked like a dream. Beresford played in 41 promotion games as Newcastle skated their way to the title and the Premier League.

Keegan warns his players they are going to get plenty of in-house competition and Beresford must have thought he had lots on his plate when the manager went out and bought the promising Watford defender Jason Drysdale for £425,000. Beresford responded to the challenge and Drysdale was still waiting to make his first-team debut when he was transferred out before the March 1995 deadline.

Probably the biggest disappointment of the season for Beresford came in the sixth round of the FA Cup. That was a match Beresford badly wanted to win, if only to erase the memory of his 1992 semi-final nightmare when he missed a shoot-out penalty against Liverpool.

Then even the consolation prize fell apart in his hands. Graeme Souness decided to buy him, agreed a deal and took him up to Anfield. A few hours later the player was in shock: he had failed the medical over a long forgotten ankle injury.

This season's quarter-final appearance at Goodison was supposed to make up for those disappointments. Newcastle were favourites against an Everton side struggling for Premiership survival. Dave Watson's goal changed all that and Beresford was not even on the pitch to see it, never mind stop it. He had limped off earlier with a hamstring injury. And they talk about the romance of the Cup!

It was a season when the England B defender was left with one crumb of comfort in that competition. He scored a fifth-round goal in the 3-1 win over Manchester City, the club that dumped him as a teenager.

# Darren Peacock

Critics might say Darren Peacock had an up-and-down season during his first campaign in Geordieland. Peacock might say, what's new? Fluctuating fortunes have been the story of his footballing life.

The big Bristol born centre-half is different, and not just because of the length of his hair which makes Barry Venison look as though he has a short back and sides. It is because of the length of his legs too.

Which other player in the land can say he is six feet one or six feet two depending on which foot he stands? Peacock has one leg longer than the other.

United fans became aware of this strange fact when Keegan made him Newcastle's most expensive player in March 1993. Queens Park Rangers, who bought him from Hereford for £200,000, made quite a profit. The fee was £2.7 million. Peacock tried to take it all in his stride but there was always the suspicion that the price tag weighed heavily.

Newcastle are a real footballing side but, like a lot of big fellows, Peacock does not always find the ball a good companion. Still, there was a strong feeling on Tyneside that he might buckle under the pressure, Peasy was still going strong at the end of the season, and his partnership with Steve Howey looked an effective one.

Things have seldom been straightforward for a defender whom former QPR boss Gerry Francis was reluctant to lose. Look at his CV.

He had trials with Bristol City and Bristol Rovers as a youngster and neither signed him on. So he joined Newport County and his League career collapsed almost before it got off the ground.

While he was recovering from a broken leg Newport, deep in financial trouble, dropped out of the League! He played a few games for them in the GM Vauxhall Conference before being given a free.

But that broken right leg caused him untold problems. When they took the plaster off they did not realise one of the bones was still broken. When the problem was discovered it was feared he would never play again. Thanks to a clever designer, who made him a specially raised boot, he did play again and it was at Hereford that his career flourished. He made 59 League appearances for them before moving to Loftus Road and suddenly the boot of misfortune was on the other foot.

Barry Venison struck a blow for the Thirty Something Brigade early

# Barry Venison

in the season when he won his first England cap. That call-up says much about the way Newcastle have been transformed under Kevin Keegan's managership.

It also says something about Venison: the older he has become, the better he has performed as a footballer. His ability to go on developing at an age when many players look as though they are feeling the strain has been remarkable.

Pound for pound – and Andy Cole's £7 million rating makes him the obvious comparison – Venison has been the best Keegan investment of all. He cost £250,000 from Liverpool in July 1992 and Newcastle have had their money back several times over.

The United manager bought him as a full-back to help with the promotion drive but he has proved truly multi-purpose. He has looked more than useful operating as a second centre-half and in a class of his own when deployed in the midfield holding role which is where Terry Venables elected to use him against the United States at Wembley in September 1994. Venison, picked again more recently against Uruguay, must have done well. Even Jimmy Hill was impressed!

But in many ways Wembley was where it started for the snappiest dresser in the Newcastle dressing-room. Remember how he found his way into the record books in May 1985? He led Sunderland out against Norwich in the Milk Cup final and at 20 became the youngest ever Wembley skipper. But for an injury picked up at Liverpool in September, he would probably have boasted an ever present record for Newcastle.

Although he surrendered the captaincy to Peter Beardsley, Keegan says Venison is just about the first name he pencils on the team sheet.

Sportswriters are not surprised, which is why they voted him the North East's Player of the Year. Improvement is the name of Venison's game. He finished third in the 1994 poll.

# Ruel Fox

When Ruel Fox breezed into St. James' Park in February 1994, he had a lot to live up to. Kevin Keegan rated the Norwich winger highly enough to smash Newcastle's transfer record to get him: a little matter of £2.25 million.

Like almost any wide player Fox can frustrate. But Keegan says he will just get better and so far that is precisely how it has worked out.

He made his Newcastle debut at Wimbledon where, despite two Peter Beardsley goals, United lost 4-2. But Fox, Chris Sutton's big mate in their Carrow Road days, did not have to wait long to produce his first goal. There were seven to share out when Swindon turned up to endure a 7-1 slaughtering and he got one. That was one of the victories which helped Newcastle finish in third place in their first season back in the big time, thereby qualifying for the Uefa Cup.

United were breaking new ground but Fox seemed to know the way, and for good reason. The previous season he had helped the Canaries negotiate two rounds of the same competition before narrowly coming to grief at the hands of Inter Milan.

That season he finished with two goals in 13 starts and collected an England B cap following a 4-2 win over Northern Ireland at Hillsborough. But Keegan always argued there was another dimension and was adamant Fox had real scoring potential.

That claim was supported this season when he comfortably worked his way into double figures. His first goal of the new campaign was registered on September 10 in a 4-2 win over Chelsea, when Newcastle took temporary charge of the Premiership's top spot. It was quickly followed by another at Arsenal where United notched their seventh league win in a row. When they used the Coca-Cola to extend a winning streak at the expense of First Division Barnsley he rattled in another.

# *Robert Lee*

Robert Lee's 1994-95 campaign should be remembered for the night he became an England international – and what a debut it turned out to be. Terry Venables threw him in for the Wembley meeting with Romania on October 12 and Lee scored the goal that gave England a 1-1 draw. What could be more memorable?

Yet some will also think about a Good Friday match at Everton which Newcastle lost 2-0. Lee, so laid back he could have made Gary Lineker look like a hatchet man, was sent off for the first time in his senior career.

He could not believe it and anyone who has encountered Lee would struggle to imagine this player being dismissed, even for two bookable offences. Yet if those two nights were of deep contrast for the 28-year-old, maybe they somehow summed up his season.

It started so well that his goals were in double figures before October and so deadly was the finishing, he was even outscoring Andy Cole. In nine seasons at Charlton Athletic the football world seemed to regard him as an orthodox winger. While that was how Keegan used him after signing him from Charlton for £700,000 in September 1992, he soon looked too good all round to be left working a line.

Perhaps his most deadly display of finishing was exhibited when Newcastle launched their European campaign against Royal Antwerp. Lee plundered a hat-trick as the Magpies raced to a 5-0 first-leg win.

When the formalities were completed a fortnight later on Tyneside, he scored another as the aggregate victory soared to 10-2. Such form was the reason Lee went on to earn his second England cap against Nigeria at Wembley in November. He looked set for an amazing season. But the second half was not quite so glorious for a player who was so unsure about his ability to settle in the North that he negotiated an escape clause in his contract.

Injury did not help and neither did Newcastle's unsure away form. But the bottom line was, that despite a season full of high spots, Lee's phenomenal story of success in the 1994-95 campaign did not run quite as long as he intended.

# Paul Bracewell

Paul Bracewell's season did not start until Boxing Day when United played a goalless draw at Leeds. What made Bracewell's day was that it started at all.

Few England internationals have had careers so blighted by injury as the former Everton midfielder.

He has had so many operations, chiefly on his ankles but also on his groin, that he ought to be sponsored by BUPA.

That is what made Bracewell's appearance at Elland Road so reassuring. He feared he would be forced to sit out the whole season. Indeed, there was a time when he thought he might not play again. When doctors discovered a growth in his groin area, a cancer scare was briefly raised but the fears were unfounded.

Yet when The Iceman, so called because he puts his feet in a bucket of the stuff after every match, looked back at Newcastle's season, one date stood out: Sunday, March 12, the day Newcastle went out of the FA Cup, losing the quarter-final to Everton by a single goal.

Bracewell, who began his career with his home town club of Stoke City, had big Wembley hopes, and for good reasons. He has made it to the FA Cup final four times, on three occasions with Everton and once with Sunderland whom he skippered against Liverpool in 1992. On each occasion he finished on the losing side.

To add insult to injury, he got his hands on the piece of soccer silver he had craved. A mix-up in the Wembley ceremony meant that Sunderland were given the wrong medals after Liverpool had beaten the Roker side with goals from Ian Rush and Michael Thomas. Players spotted the error and exchanged them back down on the pitch.

It was a pity because it would complete what some footballers regard as the full set: a League championship, a European Cup Winners' Cup and two from the Charity Shield.

After 17 seasons in the game – two of which were spent overcoming a career-threatening ankle injury – that Everton defeat left the dream agonisingly unfulfilled.

# Lee Clark

Lee Clark would not pretend that 1995 was his best year in football. He could easily consider it his most traumatic.

In many ways the former England schoolboy international is the Tynesider all young Tynesiders want to be. How many other players in the land first support the club from the terraces and then become a star in the team? That sums up the story of Clark's life and short career – or it did until his star began to wane a little.

For a young footballer who never wanted to play for anyone else it was too much to take. That is why he was almost in tears at the turn of the year. Kevin Keegan wanted him to sign a new contract. Clark was keen too. What the product of the famous Wallsend Boys' Club couldn't quite handle was sitting on the subs' bench.

He is a player who really believes in himself. Capped regularly by England as a schoolboy, he has also represented his country at youth and Under-21 level. But, if the down-grading was frustrating, there was more to follow in a difficult season. Perhaps his most eye-catching contribution came in the FA Cup third round replay at Blackburn's Ewood Park on January 18. Newcastle were second favourites to go through and without injured skipper Peter Beardsley. But thanks to a spectacular winner from Clark they won 2-1.

Despite that important goal and the zest of his game, Clark – by common assent the club's most enthusiastic worker in the community at large – could not convince Keegan he deserved to start more games. The manager's answer was straightforward: Clark had to recognise he was in direct competition with Beardsley and Robert Lee. The irony of this was that Clark was the player Beardsley took under his wing when the youngster was setting out in professional football.

Clark must have thought it never rains but it pours. Rated at £2 million plus by his manager, he failed to land a move before the March transfer deadline. The most positive inquiry came from Norwich boss John Deehan. But Deehan did not have enough money to do a deal.

If that was disappointing, so was the close to the season. Clark had turned out for Newcastle's reserve team against York City on April 20 and was carried off after two minutes with damaged knee ligaments.

# Scott Sellars

Scott Sellars will look back on Newcastle United's second season in the Premiership and feel sure it helped him play the best football of his life. Firmly established as one of the best left-sided midfield players in the game, he was being talked about as the next in a string of Keegan players to win an England call-up. It all came to shuddering halt on October 18, the night Newcastle aimed to extend their Uefa Cup run and missed. They were playing the return leg of a second-round tie with Athletic Bilbao, and with only a 3-2 advantage they needed to keep a clean sheet over in Spain. They lost 1-0 and Sellars' world collapsed too. The stabbing pain he experienced a few days earlier against Manchester United returned with a vengeance and warned him to expect the worst. He hobbled off and was replaced by Lee Clark.

"One moment I was in the best form of my life," he said, "and the next it seemed my entire future as a football player was on the line."

There were some grim faces around St. James' Park as Sheffield-born Sellars returned home to see a knee specialist. He'd suffered severe damage and was told there was only one real option: complete rest.

Keegan was determined the player he had bought from Leeds for £700,000 in the spring of 1993 would not become an outcast when United were flying in the League. So he got him involved with the backroom staff. Sellars knew first hand that 'on the outside' feeling and did not care for it. He had experienced it at Leeds in his second spell with the Yorkshire club. He made around 80 appearances for Leeds as a youngster before being sold for £20,000 to Blackburn, where he spent six happy seasons. He was part of that Rovers team which always made the play-offs but could never quite manage promotion until Kenny Dalglish arrived.

Dalglish was appointed early in the 1991-92 season which ended with Blackburn winning the play-off final against Leicester at Wembley. Sellars was not to know that was his last game for Rovers.

He had been offered a two-year contract but wanted three years. Before he knew it he had been sold back to Leeds for £800,000. What should have been a glittering return turned out to be as dull as ditchwater as far as he was concerned. He was hardly given a game by Howard Wilkinson.

# Andy Cole

Inside a couple of years Andy Cole established himself as a footballing institution on Tyneside. He was the most successful goalscorer Newcastle United have ever had. That is not opinion, it is cold fact.

So there were bound to be shock waves when Keegan took the extraordinary decision to sell him to Manchester United in January.

If logic was being applied, there seemed two flaws in the sale. First, the manager did not have a replacement lined up. Perhaps worse, he was selling the club's most reliable scorer to a championship rival.

No wonder Keegan admitted: "I am well aware there's a bullet with my name on it if I've got it wrong. Whether or not the trigger is pulled depends entirely on how well this club does in the future".

Newcastle fans, particularly those opposed to the sale, knew how Newcastle had done in the past with Cole. From the moment Cole arrived in March 1993, he made himself at home: 12 appearances in the promotion season and 12 goals scored.

If that was tasty stuff from a finisher signed from Bristol City for £1.75 million, it was only the hors d'oeuvre. Cole, filled with the desire to be England's No 1, set about dismantling Newcastle's all-time scoring record.

By April 27 he became the first United player to score 40 goals in a season – he finished with 41 – when he scored the third goal in a 5-1 win over Aston Villa, smashing the previous record held jointly by the Fifties hero George Robledo and Hughie Gallacher.

Yet, if that seemed to set the Nottingham-born striker up for life at Newcastle, the following season was to show how quickly things change.

Cole scored on the opening day of the new season in a 3-1 win at Leicester. But five months and 14 goals later the love affair was over.

The record-breaking transfer started when Keegan asked Alex Ferguson about his young Irish winger Keith Gillespie. One thing led to another and the British record transfer deal was concluded at a Sheffield hotel. Cole was history as far as Newcastle were concerned.

The book was closed on a phenomenal 22-month story, amidst much controversy. In 84 appearances in a black and white shirt Handy Andy came up with 68 goals. It was quite a performance.

# Peter Beardsley

Peter Beardsley has picked up a few nicknames on his journey to the top of his chosen trade. His latest one is "Stan". Newcastle players re-christened him after Keegan predicted his skipper was looking so lively at 34, he could do a Stanley Matthews and play to 50.

Who knows what Beardsley can do? He continues to astound everyone with super goals and subtle play. When Keegan brought him back in the summer of 1993, the United chairman thought his manager had taken leave of his senses – £1.3m for a 32 year-old! Keegan simply said: "Wait and see."

As Sir John Hall has long since admitted, his manager was absolutely right. Beardsley showed straight away that he was pure genius, scoring 24 goals in his first season and making a hefty slice of the 41 by Andy Cole. And that was after he had missed the early part of the season recovering from a fractured cheekbone sustained in an Anfield testimonial clash with Liverpool's Neil Ruddock.

What is more, the move involved Keegan making "Stan" a promise and it was kept. The manager and his assistant Terry McDermott assured him that by returning to Tyneside he would get back into the England team. They were so certain they even struck a bet. Sure enough, on March 9, 1994 Terry Venables gave the former Liverpool and Everton favourite his 50th cap against Denmark at Wembley.

It is not the number of goals Beardsley scores but the way he produces the spectacular ones that make him different. There are several contenders for his goal of the season, but many think the one he produced on April 8 will take some beating. It was his 14th of the season and left young Norwich keeper Andy Marshall sick.

Beardsley picked up the ball 30 yards out, wide on the right. He shaped to cross, waited for Marshall to 'steal' a yard in anticipation of a ball to the far post and, with the outside of his right boot, sent it screaming in at the the near post.

It was a bad goal for the Norwich boss John Deehan too. Little more than 24 hours later, he quit the sinking Premiership club.

It was also the sort of goal which makes Newcastle fans wish their prodigal son had never left Newcastle for Liverpool in 1986.

# Paul Kitson

Paul Kitson finished the season with enough goals in the bag to satisfy any self-respecting striker. What he did not quite end up with was the full approval of Geordie fans and, for centre-forwards hoping to find a place in the club's hall of fame that is bad news.

In one sense Kitson became a victim of football's version of musical chairs. When the music stopped, and Andy Cole departed to Manchester United, someone was caught sitting in Cole's chair.

That was Kitson and he was bound to suffer by the comparison. Circumstances projected him as Cole's replacement even though he was signed from Derby County long before Cole was sold for £7 million. In short, he always looked to be a loser.

His cause was probably not helped either by events surrounding his £2.5m arrival from the Baseball Ground. Newcastle went to an awful lot of trouble to get him, setting up and pushing through a deal that County owner Lionel Pickering initially blocked.

On Thursday September 22, 1994 he turned up at St James' Park for signing talks that were thought to be routine. Hours later he was on his way back to the Midlands having failed to agree terms.

The following morning headlines featuring the word "greedy" screamed out at him even though Keegan had suggested no such thing. Though he eventually accepted Newcastle's offer, his image had taken a battering before he even kicked a ball for his new club.

It was as well there were a few friendly faces around his new club. Keegan's aide Arthur Cox, who had bought him for Derby from Leicester City for £1.3 million was one.

Kitson, troubled by injury early in the campaign, scored his first United goal on October 26 in a 2-0 Coca-Cola Cup win over Manchester United. He followed that with another in a 2-1 home win over QPR and came up with his first away goal in a 3-2 defeat by Wimbledon. Though he kept plugging away, it was still a hard slog.

But Cox has shown no signs of losing faith. "I liked him the first time I saw him as a 16-year-old in Leicester's A team," he says. "There was just something about him. You get the feeling with some kids that they have the ability to reach the top."

# Keith Gillespie

Keith Gillespie arrived as the £1m makeweight in the £7 million Andy Cole deal with Manchester United.

While he was very much an unknown quantity as far as the fans were concerned, Keegan gave him a great build-up: the most exciting player he had spotted since returning to football.

The Northern Ireland youngster responded with a super home debut on January 25 against Wimbledon. It would be nice to say he maintained that standard but not entirely accurate.

# Robbie Elliott

This should have been a big year for 21-year-old Elliott. That it wasn't was wholly down to atrocious luck rather than poor play. The Gosforth-born youngster is probably the unluckiest player on the books. He started the season suffering from shin splints and ended with serious knee ligament damage, a tragic development for a full-back who already has a history of cruciate ligament problems. The knee problem flared up after he had scored an outstanding goal in the Easter Monday home defeat by Leeds.

# Steve Watson

Newcastle's action man did not get nearly as much first-team action as his talent suggested he would. Yet the England Under-21 defender remains a big favourite with the fans. He made his Newcastle name when he won and held down a first-team place as a 16-year-old.

At the start of the season he kept the Swiss international Marc Hottiger out of the side but that supremacy did not last.

# Alex Mathie

In another era Mathie might have become a big goalscoring name at St James'. But Mathie, bought from Morton by Keegan, found himself competing with Andy Cole and Peter Beardsley for a front-line place. Keegan sold him to Ipswich just before the deadline for £500,000.

# Alan Neilson

Born in Germany, the son of a serviceman but a Welsh international defender, Neilson found himself in an odd spot: good enough for his country but not for his club. But his competitive style meant that in the handful of games he did have in the Premiership he was never in danger of letting anyone down.

# Mike Hooper

Hooper was brought in from Liverpool for £550,000 to replace Pavel Srnicek. But, when the Czech responded to the challenge, Hooper – a keen birdwatcher – did not match him. The result was that first team appearances were restricted, which was hugely discouraging for a keeper who thought his days of being the back-up man were over when he left Anfield.

# Kevin Keegan

Kevin Keegan opened the 1994-95 campaign with one thought on his mind.  He had just given Newcastle their best season since 1927, finishing in third place in the club's first season back in the big league. He took stock, looked forward, and set himself a target. "The priority now is to win a trophy," he said, "and then win another." He clearly believed that would quickly be achieved because as a team and a club, Newcastle were hot stuff. Yet, when Keegan looked back at the season in May, he found the Magpies were not in the driving seat at all. They fell way short in the race for the title, drifted out of Europe and the Coca-Cola Cup and finally pinned all their hopes on winning the FA Cup. But on a sorry Sunday at Goodison that dream went out of the window too as Dave Watson shot Everton through to the semi-finals.

Somehow, in the remaining months of the season, Keegan never looked the same or sounded it either. People who know him really well say the process of defeat absolutely chokes him. During the final throes of this campaign, it did.

However, if the dream was damaged, Keegan's image was not in the eyes of fans. Geordies can hardly forget, and really should not, how he has transformed their club in partnership with the hard-edged chairman Sir John Hall.

They were drifting into the old Third Division when he took on his first managerial appointment in February 1992, a successor to the ill-fated Ossie Ardiles. Not only did he turn that crisis around but the following season Newcastle soared to promotion and into the Premiership where they thrived still further.

Given the situation they were in, this was fantasy football from a team dubbed "the Entertainers" by the producers of BSkyB.

That is why fingers did not point accusingly in his direction this season. He even took the biggest risk of his career by selling Andy Cole and survived it by winning public backing. One former United manager would have been astounded. When, in the seventies, Gordon Lee sold scoring idol Malcolm Macdonald to Arsenal for £330,000, a lot of fans could not forgive him.

Lee left. Keegan is definitely staying.

# The Future

The future looks glittering for a club inspired by chairman Sir John Hall's strong leadership behind the scenes and fronted by Kevin Keegan's charismatic brand of management. The trick will be taking it off the drawing board and transposing the grand plan on to the playing fields of Europe. That is where Hall wants to be and, as the record shows, he is the sort of man who usually gets what he wants.

He believes some kind of European Super League is inevitable, and is adamant Newcastle will be a part of it. Yet, while Newcastle are undoubtedly establishing themselves as one of the game's big spenders, the nuts and bolts of their future may well be put together a few miles from St James' Park, on a 325-acre site called Woolsington Hall Farm, just down the runway from Newcastle Airport.

That is where United are to site the revolutionary sports academy which is to bear the name of the club's late chairman, Stan Seymour, a man always passionate about the business of developing young talent. The aim is to establish the Woolsington Hall site as the finest training facility in Europe where scores of young footballers will be developed. Like most things that happen at United, it is Hall's "baby" and it is his way of investing positively in the club's future. Hall believes firmly that all top businesses must be supported by extensive research and development operations. This, he says, is Newcastle United's. The chairman laid down this promise when he showed club employees around the site last season: "This centre will be the best in Europe." The centre, part of a £12m development, will boast major indoor facilities, two full-size pitches, a range of junior practice pitches and an 18-hole golf course. The administrative block will be housed in the former manor style residence, Woolsington Hall.

Extensions to existing buildings will pave the way for conference, lecture and seminar rooms and even en suite bedrooms for young players who want to stay there. There will also be a top sports injury clinic, leisure facilities, swimming pool, bar, rest rooms, golf clubhouse and even a creche.

The purpose is to provide an environment geared to giving stars of the future the start they could otherwise only dream of. It all comes under the giant black-and-white umbrella of the Newcastle Sporting Club. So, while Newcastle will always be active in the transfer market as they aspire to be a top European outfit, they will also be in a position to dip into their reservoir of home-grown talent.

Initially the operation will come under the control of Chris McMenemy, son of Lawrie, who is earmarked to be the first director of the Soccer Academy. Hall, though, likes to plan ahead and, when club skipper Peter Beardsley eventually retires as a player, he is to have a pivotal academy role. Beardsley, a non-smoking, teetotaller, is seen as the perfect role model for young Geordies.

Keegan, however, cannot guarantee when he will be in a position to release the England international for such duties. Even though Beardsley is 34, his manager expects him to play on for several seasons.

The future, of course, revolves around Keegan's presence as well. And while management is a transient occupation, Hall believes his team boss is firmly bolted down.

The chairman never thought simply in terms of three or even five years, which is marathon by soccer standards for Keegan's contract. He reckoned, if he was to develop Newcastle's commercial future fully then he needed to make the ex-England captain a permanent fixture. That is why he was cock-a-hoop when he announced that his manager had signed a 10-year contract that would tie him to the club until the year 2004.

While the rewards for such an agreement will re-inforce Keegan's millionaire status, they should unquestionably help Newcastle to become richer and more successful.

Though Keegan has yet to provide Newcastle with their first championship success since the '20s, he, too, sees Europe as the major goal. Keegan got a taste for Europe again, having played in European competition for some years, when his side qualified for the '94-'95 Uefa Cup and he immediately got the appetite for more.

Yet Keegan would never tire of reminding anyone that the future of any club is in its players. While he can still pull in a superstar's autograph queue and he will sign every last one he is a believer in players being the biggest stars.

Looking to the future, he can see he already has several in the making and that is before the academy gets off the ground. Some already have made their way into Newcastle's first team.

Steve Watson, a Wallsend lad, has the energy, enterprise and talent to become one. He broke into the first team as a 16-year-old and is  firmly established as an England Under-21 international. Robbie Elliott, also a defender, looks to have a big future, too, particularly if he can avoid the sort of injuries that have marred the early stages of his career. Elliott has had enough operations to last him an entire career. Diamonds are found below the surface which is where, in footballing terms, the young Tynesider Paul Brayson lies. If Andy Cole was United's last golden boot, then a lot of good judges believe the slightly built striker could be the next. In junior and reserve team games he can not stop scoring and was even included in the Uefa Cup squad for last season's tie with Athletic Bilbao. He is a little player with a big future and arrived at United after playing for a team coached by the Newcastle midfield player Lee Clark.

# Acknowledgements

Newcastle United
History by John David
PenPictures by John Donoghue
Future by John Donoghue

Thanks to Daily Express Chief Soccer Writer Steve Curry.
North Eastern Soccer Correspondent, John Donoghue and other members
of the Express team: John Wragg, Jim Holden, Kevin Moseley,
Richard Lewis, Matt Dickinson, John Keith and John Bean.

Also to Frances Jennings for sorting out the system and
providing the disks and to Matthew Emery for picture research.

With grateful thanks to
Bill Chalmers at HarperCollins*Manufacturing*
Ron Taylor at Keene Repro,
Colin Eyre at The Imaging Business,
Jeremy Alexander and Tom Gorham
for all their help and expertise


All pictures used are from the library of
Express Newspapers plc.